CONGRESSIONAL POLICIES, PRACTICES AND PROCEDURES

CONGRESS AND THE EUROPEAN PARLIAMENT: LEGISLATIVE COOPERATION

CONGRESSIONAL POLICIES, PRACTICES AND PROCEDURES

Additional books in this series can be found on Nova's website under the Series tab.

Additional E-books in this series can be found on Nova's website under the E-book tab.

LAWS AND LEGISLATION

Additional books in this series can be found on Nova's website under the Series tab.

Additional E-books in this series can be found on Nova's website under the E-book tab.

CONGRESSIONAL POLICIES, PRACTICES AND PROCEDURES

CONGRESS AND THE EUROPEAN PARLIAMENT: LEGISLATIVE COOPERATION

DEVON J. ARMSTRONG
AND
NEIL T. FITZSIMMONS
EDITORS

Nova Science Publishers, Inc.
New York

Copyright © 2012 by Nova Science Publishers, Inc.

All rights reserved. No part of this book may be reproduced, stored in a retrieval system or transmitted in any form or by any means: electronic, electrostatic, magnetic, tape, mechanical photocopying, recording or otherwise without the written permission of the Publisher.

For permission to use material from this book please contact us:
Telephone 631-231-7269; Fax 631-231-8175
Web Site: http://www.novapublishers.com

NOTICE TO THE READER

The Publisher has taken reasonable care in the preparation of this book, but makes no expressed or implied warranty of any kind and assumes no responsibility for any errors or omissions. No liability is assumed for incidental or consequential damages in connection with or arising out of information contained in this book. The Publisher shall not be liable for any special, consequential, or exemplary damages resulting, in whole or in part, from the readers' use of, or reliance upon, this material. Any parts of this book based on government reports are so indicated and copyright is claimed for those parts to the extent applicable to compilations of such works.

Independent verification should be sought for any data, advice or recommendations contained in this book. In addition, no responsibility is assumed by the publisher for any injury and/or damage to persons or property arising from any methods, products, instructions, ideas or otherwise contained in this publication.

This publication is designed to provide accurate and authoritative information with regard to the subject matter covered herein. It is sold with the clear understanding that the Publisher is not engaged in rendering legal or any other professional services. If legal or any other expert assistance is required, the services of a competent person should be sought. FROM A DECLARATION OF PARTICIPANTS JOINTLY ADOPTED BY A COMMITTEE OF THE AMERICAN BAR ASSOCIATION AND A COMMITTEE OF PUBLISHERS.

Additional color graphics may be available in the e-book version of this book.

Library of Congress Cataloging-in-Publication Data

Congress and the European Parliament : legislative cooperation / editors, Devon J. Armstrong and Neil T. Fitzsimmons.
    p. cm.
  Includes index.
  "CRS Report for Congress"
  ISBN 978-1-62100-748-7 (softcover)
 1. United States. Congress. 2. European Parliament. 3. Legislation--United States--International cooperation. 4. Legislation--European Union countries--International cooperation. I. Armstrong, Devon J. II. Fitzsimmons, Neil T. III. Library of Congress. Congressional Research Service.
  JK1021.C5527 2011
  328.73'0745--dc23
                            2011038324

Published by Nova Science Publishers, Inc. † New York

CONTENTS

Preface		**vii**
Chapter 1	The U.S. Congress and the European Parliament: Evolving Transatlantic Legislative Cooperation *Kristin Archick and Vincent Morelli*	1
Chapter 2	The European Parliament *Kristin Archick and Derek E. Mix*	41
Index		**63**

PREFACE

The United States and the European Union (EU) share an extensive, dynamic, and for many a mutually beneficial political and economic partnership. A growing element of that relationship is the role that the U.S. Congress and the European Parliament (EP) have begun to play, including in areas ranging from foreign and economic policy to regulatory reform.Consequently, some officials and experts on both sides of the Atlantic have asked whether it would be beneficial for Congress and the EP to strengthen institutional ties further and to explore the possibility of coordinating efforts to develop more complementary policies in some areas. This book discusses the transatlantic legislative cooperation between the United States Congress and the European Parliament.

Chapter 1- The United States and the European Union (EU) share an extensive, dynamic, and for many a mutually beneficial political and economic partnership. A growing element of that relationship is the role that the U.S. Congress and the European Parliament (EP)—a key EU institution—have begun to play, including in areas ranging from foreign and economic policy to regulatory reform. Consequently, some officials and experts on both sides of the Atlantic have asked whether it would be beneficial for Congress and the EP to strengthen institutional ties further and to explore the possibility of coordinating efforts to develop more complementary policies in some areas.

The Transatlantic Legislators' Dialogue (TLD), the formal exchange between Congress (actually the House of Representatives) and the European Parliament, was launched in 1999, although semi-annual meetings between Congress and the EP date back to 1972. Recently, the TLD's visibility has increased following the 2007 decision to name it as an advisor to the Transatlantic Economic Council (TEC), which seeks to "advance the work of reducing or eliminating non-tariff barriers to transatlantic commerce and trade." Proponents of establishing closer relations between the U.S. Congress and the EP also point to the Parliament's growing influence as a result of the EU's new Lisbon Treaty, which took effect in December 2009. The Lisbon Treaty has increased the relative power of the EP within the EU, and in some cases, with significant implications for U.S. interests—as seen by the EP's initial rejection in February 2010 of the U.S.-EU terrorist finance tracking agreement (known as the SWIFT accord).

Chapter 2- The 736-member European Parliament (EP) is a key institution of the European Union (EU), a unique political and economic partnership composed of 27 member states. The EP is the only EU institution that is directly elected. The EP plays a role in the EU's legislative and budgeting processes, and works closely with the two other main EU bodies, the European Commission and the Council of the European Union (also known as the Council of Ministers). Although the EP does not formally initiate EU legislation, it shares legislative power with the Council of Ministers in many policy areas, giving it the right to accept, amend, or reject proposed EU laws.

Members of the European Parliament (MEPs) serve five-year terms. The most recent EP elections were held in June 2009. The EP currently has seven political groups, which caucus according to political ideology rather than nationality, plus a number of "non-attached" or independent members. The EP has 20 standing committees that are key actors in the adoption of EU legislation and a total of 41 delegations that maintain international parliament-to-parliament relations. The EP is led by a President, who oversees its work and represents the EP externally.

In: Congress and the European Parliament
Editors D. J. Armstrong et al.
ISBN: 978-1-62100-748-7
©2012 Nova Science Publishers, Inc.

Chapter 1

THE U.S. CONGRESS AND THE EUROPEAN PARLIAMENT: EVOLVING TRANSATLANTIC LEGISLATIVE COOPERATION[1]

Kristin Archick and Vincent Morelli

SUMMARY

The United States and the European Union (EU) share an extensive, dynamic, and for many a mutually beneficial political and economic partnership. A growing element of that relationship is the role that the U.S. Congress and the European Parliament (EP)—a key EU institution—have begun to play, including in areas ranging from foreign and economic policy to regulatory reform. Consequently, some officials and experts on both sides of the Atlantic have asked whether it would be beneficial for Congress and the EP to strengthen institutional ties further and to explore the possibility of coordinating efforts to develop more complementary policies in some areas.

The Transatlantic Legislators' Dialogue (TLD), the formal exchange between Congress (actually the House of Representatives) and the European Parliament, was launched in 1999, although semi-annual meetings between

---

[1] This is an edited, reformatted and augmented version of Congressional Research Service R41552.

Congress and the EP date back to 1972. Recently, the TLD's visibility has increased following the 2007 decision to name it as an advisor to the Transatlantic Economic Council (TEC), which seeks to "advance the work of reducing or eliminating non-tariff barriers to transatlantic commerce and trade." Proponents of establishing closer relations between the U.S. Congress and the EP also point to the Parliament's growing influence as a result of the EU's new Lisbon Treaty, which took effect in December 2009. The Lisbon Treaty has increased the relative power of the EP within the EU, and in some cases, with significant implications for U.S. interests—as seen by the EP's initial rejection in February 2010 of the U.S.-EU terrorist finance tracking agreement (known as the SWIFT accord).

Over the last few years, in part because of the TLD's new TEC-related responsibilities, some Members of Congress have suggested that there is a need for more cooperation with the EP, and have raised questions with respect to how this might best be accomplished. For those Members and outside advocates of closer relations, questions have surfaced about whether the TLD itself should be reorganized, how the standing committees in both institutions might interact, and what role, if any, for the U.S. Senate. Throughout 2010 contacts between Congress and the Parliament increased in frequency, including at the committee level. However, many observers note that the EP has been far out in front of Congress in pursuit of a stronger relationship. In 2010, the Parliament opened a liaison office in Washington, charged with keeping the EP better informed of legislative activity in Congress and vice-versa. In addition, each EP standing committee has named a "TLD Administrator" on its staff to act as a contact point between the committee and the TLD, as well as between the committee and its counterpart committee in the U.S. Congress.

While there appears to be no formal opposition within Congress to increasing contacts with the European Parliament, some point out that with the exception of a few Members with previous experience in the TLD, Congress as a whole has been seen at best ambivalent to such efforts and has not demonstrated as much enthusiasm as the EP about forging closer relations. This observation had been noted by the EP itself since the beginning of the 112th Congress given that neither the new Chair nor the Vice-Chair of the USTLD were announced until early June.

This report provides background on the Congress–EP relationship and the role of the TLD. It also explores potential future options should an effort to strengthen ties between the two bodies gain momentum.

INTRODUCTION

The U.S.-EU Relationship

The United States Congress and successive U.S. administrations have long supported the European Union (EU) as a way to advance democracy and strong economic partners in Europe. The current 27-member EU is the latest stage in a process of European integration begun in the 1950s to promote lasting peace and prosperity on the European continent.[1] During the Cold War, the United States viewed this European integration project as central to deterring the Soviet threat by securing free markets and engendering political stability in Europe.

Despite the end of the Cold War, many observers assert that the security and prosperity of the United States and the EU remain inextricably linked. Both the United States and the EU face a common set of challenges—from countering terrorism and weapons proliferation to slowing environmental degradation to ensuring the stability of international financial markets—and have few other comparable partners with whom they share such similar interests and values. Proponents of close U.S.-EU ties argue that neither side can adequately address the diverse number of global concerns alone, and that the United States and the EU have a proven track record of working together. For example, the United States and the EU are promoting security in the Balkans and Afghanistan, and have intensified law enforcement cooperation since the 2001 terrorist attacks on the United States, and have been cooperating closely to manage and contain Iran's nuclear ambitions.

Furthermore, the United States and the EU share a huge, mutually beneficial, and increasingly interdependent trade and investment relationship. Despite the recent global economic downturn, the combined U.S. and EU economies account for nearly 54% of global gross domestic product and roughly 28% of global exports and 33% of global imports. According to one recent study, the transatlantic economy generates close to $5 trillion in commercial sales a year and employs up to 15 million workers on both sides of the Atlantic. Of particular importance is the fact that U.S. and European companies are the biggest investors in each other's markets. In 2010, it is estimated that nearly $2 trillion (or 52%) of U.S. foreign direct investment (FDI) went to Europe while $1.4 trillion of EU FDI flowed to the United States.[2] Historically, U.S.-EU cooperation has also been critical in making the world trading system more open and efficient.

At the same time, the U.S.-EU relationship has been challenged in recent years by numerous foreign policy and trade conflicts. U.S.-EU relations reached a historic low in 2003 over the U.S.-led invasion of Iraq, which some EU member states supported and others strongly opposed. In the aftermath of this crisis, the former Bush Administration sought to improve cooperation and emphasize areas of partnership with the EU. In the years since, observers point out that U.S.-EU tensions on several key issues, such as Iran and the Israeli-Palestinian conflict, have dissipated. The Obama Administration has also sought to bolster ties with the EU and has introduced some policies that have helped reduce U.S.-EU frictions further; for example, many terrorist detainee and interrogation practices, which the EU had long opposed as degrading shared values, have been reversed. However, U.S.-EU differences in other areas—such as data privacy, climate change, and energy security—persist, as do U.S.-EU trade disputes over poultry, aircraft subsidies, and bio-engineered food products. Regulatory barriers to greater trade and investment also remain, despite efforts on both sides to promote regulatory cooperation.

Role of the Legislatures

In light of both the possible benefits of and challenges to greater U.S.-EU cooperation on a wide array of common political and economic issues, some Members of Congress and their counterparts in the European Parliament (EP) have recently expressed renewed interest in strengthening institutional ties and enhancing cooperation. The EP is a key institution of the European Union and the only one that is directly elected (see "Background on the European Parliament" for more information on the EP). Relations between Congress and the EP date back to 1972, and institutional cooperation currently exists through the Transatlantic Legislators' Dialogue (TLD). However, in recent years, new momentum for boosting Congressional-EP relations has come from the decision in 2007 to name the TLD as an advisor to the Transatlantic Economic Council (TEC), which was created by the United States Government and the European Union at the annual U.S.-EU summit in 2007. The TEC is aimed at reducing remaining non-tariff and regulatory barriers to transatlantic commerce and trade (see "Transatlantic Economic Council").

In addition, proponents of establishing closer relations between the U.S. Congress and the European Parliament point to the EP's growing influence following the entrance into force of the EU's new Lisbon Treaty in December 2009. Most experts agree that the Lisbon Treaty—the EU's latest effort at institutional reform—significantly increases the relative power of the EP within the EU. Among other measures, the treaty further expands the EP's role in the EU's legislative process by giving the EP a greater say over most all legislation passed in the EU, including in sensitive areas such as agriculture and justice and home affairs. The treaty also strengthens the EP's role in the EU's budgetary process, gives the EP the right to approve or reject international agreements by majority vote, and expands its decision-making authority over trade-related issues.[3]

Analysts observe that the EP has not been shy about exerting its new powers, and in some cases, with implications for U.S. interests. In February 2010, for example, the EP rejected a U.S.-EU agreement (known as the SWIFT accord) that would have continued allowing U.S. authorities access to European financial data to help counter terrorism. Prior to the Lisbon Treaty, the EP did not have the authority to veto such an accord. Although the EP eventually approved a new U.S.-EU SWIFT agreement in July 2010, it did so only after several EP demands related to strengthening data privacy protections for EU citizens were agreed to by the United States and the other EU institutions. With the Lisbon Treaty now in force, the EP must also approve a 2007 U.S.-EU agreement permitting airlines to share passenger name record (PNR) data with U.S. authorities as part of the fight against terrorism; some in the EP have long been concerned that the PNR agreement does not contain sufficient protections to safeguard the personal data and privacy rights of EU citizens. U.S. and EU officials are currently negotiating some revisions to the 2007 PNR accord in an effort to assuage EP concerns and ensure its approval.

In light of the SWIFT votes and now the PNR issue, U.S. policymakers have taken note that the EP may be an increasingly important actor in the conduct of U.S.-EU relations. In May 2010, U.S. Vice President Joseph Biden addressed the EP in Brussels. In September 2010, in a speech before the Council on Foreign Relations, U.S. Secretary of State Hillary Clinton acknowledged that the EP was now an "influential player." As such, some U.S. officials and analysts suggest that it is in U.S. interests for Congress to forge stronger ties with the EP. In November 2010, U.S. Ambassador to the EU William Kennard asserted that there is an "urgent need to intensify and deepen" the U.S. relationship with the EP, and in particular, that between Congress and the EP.[4] This message may have been heard by Congress but in a different way. Recently, reso-lutions were introduced in both Houses (and adopted in the Senate) effectively stating that Congress would not support significant changes to the PNR agreement—in direct contrast to what some in the EP have been advocating.

Many of those who support Congressional and EP aspirations to bolster relations between the two legislative bodies also point out that, in the past, there have been instances in which legislation passed by either the U.S. Congress or the EP has affected the other side and contributed to U.S.-EU tensions. For example, in 2002, the U.S. Congress passed the Sarbanes-Oxley Act to reform U.S. corporate accounting practices in the wake of a series of scandals at major corporations such as Enron. EU officials objected to many of the provisions of the act, claiming that they did not take into account differences in European corporate governance and financing mechanisms. Meanwhile, some U.S. business interests and exporters have expressed similar concerns about the costs and burdens of new EU regulations, such as those governing chemicals (known as REACH), which took effect in 2007. In 2010, U.S.-EU frictions surfaced over proposed EU legislation to regulate hedge funds and private equity groups; U.S. officials contended that some elements of the initial legislative proposal would make it more difficult for U.S. hedge funds to sell their products in the EU.

Pointing to the above examples, some experts assert that U.S.-EU tensions could have perhaps been avoided—or at least reduced—if both sides' legislative bodies had consulted more ahead of time. Many of this view recommend that the U.S. Congress and the EP should make a more concerted effort to coordinate legislation in some policy areas. In several post-TLD meeting statements, both sides have urged the creation of an "early warning" system that would alert both bodies of potential problems related to legislation working its way through either institution. In addition to financial services and regulatory issues that would be candidates for legislative cooperation, other areas that would possibly benefit from greater consultation and coordination include energy efficiency standards, energy security, data protection, and cyber-security. More recently, it has been suggested by some that as Congress begins deliberations on the reauthorization of the Farm Bill and the EP begins work on renewing the EU's Common Agriculture Policy (CAP), the two sides should consult and identify common issues in an effort to avoid potential problems that could result from emerging new policies.

Although there has not been a significant movement within Congress to expand Congress-EP relations, those in favor of boosting ties between the two institutions have proposed a variety of possible options for doing so, including increasing staff exchanges and establishing a Congressional liaison office in Brussels. Some have suggested that Congress needs a new, more institutionalized structure to manage its relationship with the EP. Others assert that a new structure is not necessary, but that the existing TLD, especially on the U.S. side, should be enhanced and reinvigorated. (For a more extensive discussion of these options and others, see "Possible Options for Future Congress-Parliament Cooperation".)

BACKGROUND ON THE EUROPEAN PARLIAMENT

The 736-member *European Parliament (EP)* is the only EU institution that is directly elected. As such, it represents the citizens of the EU. The EP plays a role in the EU's legislative and budgeting processes, and works closely with the two other main EU bodies: the *European Commission*, which represents the interests of the EU as a whole and essentially serves as the EU's executive; and the *Council of the European Union* (also known as the *Council of Ministers*), which represents the EU's 27 member states. The EP also exercises a degree of supervision over the Commission; it has more limited oversight over the activities of the Council.

The EP has accumulated more power over time. Although the European Commission has the right of legislative initiative in most cases, the EP shares legislative power with the Council of Ministers in many policy areas ranging from economics to the environment to social policy; in such areas, both the EP and the Council must approve a Commission proposal for it to become EU law in a process known as the *ordinary legislative procedure* or *co-decision*. With the entrance into force of the new Lisbon Treaty in December 2009, the Parliament's right of co-decision now applies to the majority of EU legislation (with some exceptions, such as in the areas of taxation and foreign policy).

> ***Members of the European Parliament (MEPs)*** serve five-year terms. Voting for the EP takes place on a national basis, with the number of MEPs elected in each EU member state based roughly on population size. The EP currently has ***seven political groups***, which caucus according to political ideology rather than nationality, plus a number of "non-attached" or independent members. A political group must contain at least 25 MEPs from a minimum of seven EU member states. No single group in the EP has an absolute majority, making compromise and coalition-building important elements of the legislative process.
>
> The EP's two largest groups are the center-right *European People's Party (EPP)*, with 265 seats, and the center-left *Progressive Alliance of Socialists and Democrats in the European Parliament (S&D)*, with 184 seats. The other EP groups are: the centrist *Alliance of Liberals and Democrats for Europe (ALDE)*, with 85 seats; the leftist and pro-environment *Greens/European Free Alliance (Greens-EFA)*, with 55 seats; the right-wing, anti-federalist *European Conservatives and Reformists (ECR)*, with 54 seats; the far-left *European United Left/Nordic Green Left (GUE/NGL)*, with 35 seats; and the euroskeptic *Europe of Freedom and Democracy (EFD)*, with 30 seats.
>
> Every two-and-a-half years (twice per parliamentary term), MEPs vote to elect a ***President of the European Parliament*** to oversee its work and to represent the EP externally. The EP has ***20 standing committees*** that are key actors in the adoption of EU legislation and ***41 delegations*** that maintain international parliament-to-parliament relations. A ***Secretariat*** of approximately 5,000 non-partisan civil servants provides administrative and technical support to the Parliament. MEPs and political groups also have their own staff assistants.
>
> Strasbourg, France, is the official seat of the EP; this location, close to the border with Germany, was chosen to symbolize peace and reconciliation in Europe. Plenary sessions are held in Strasbourg once a month. The work of the EP is also carried out in Brussels, Belgium, where the standing committees meet and where occasional part-plenary sessions are held, and in Luxembourg, where some sections of the EP's Secretariat are based.

On the other hand, although there has not been an observable opposition to such an enhanced relationship, skeptics doubt the utility or need to establish a stronger relationship between the U.S. Congress and the European Parliament. They note that despite the increased powers granted to the EP in the Lisbon Treaty, the two bodies are not exactly comparable. Unlike the U.S. Congress, the EP does not have the right of legislative initiative; in most cases, that right rests with the European Commission, which functions as the EU's executive. And although the EP can accept, amend, or reject proposed EU legislation, it shares these powers with the Council of the European Union (also called the Council of Ministers), which represents the 27 member states.

Given the structural and procedural differences between Congress and the EP, some question whether the two bodies could effectively work together on legislative issues. In addition, some Members and their counterparts in the EP have very different views on issues such as climate change or energy policy. Moreover, many point out that neither Congress nor the EP would likely be inclined toward devising or approving legislation that takes into account the interests of the transatlantic relationship at the potential expense of their own constituents. Finally, most Members of Congress—other than those involved in the TLD—have not expressed as much interest or enthusiasm as their counterparts in the EP regarding establishing closer legislative coordination or cooperation.

DEVELOPMENT OF RELATIONS BETWEEN THE U.S. CONGRESS AND THE EUROPEAN PARLIAMENT

As noted above, formal exchanges between the U.S. House of Representatives and the European Parliament can be traced back to 1972, when a group of Members of the House traveled to Brussels for the express purpose of meeting and exchanging views with the Parliament. At the time, Congress viewed the then-European Community (the precursor to the modern day EU) mostly as a commercial and trade arrangement with the ability to negotiate trade agreements, but the EP was an institution with limited visibility and unknown authority. The first congressional visits to Brussels appear to have been arranged by Members of the House Committee on Ways and Means who were interested in issues such as agriculture subsidies, steel tariffs, anti-dumping initiatives, and general trade-related areas. These initial parliamentary contacts, which only involved the House of Representatives, became known as the United States-European Community Interparliamentary Group. Beginning sometime after these early exchanges, with few exceptions, Members of the House and members of the European Parliament (MEPs) have met formally twice a year, once in the United States and once in Europe.

Given the evolving nature of the transatlantic relationship, and the changes taking place within the EU itself, the purpose and focus of the Congress–EP interparliamentary exchange gradually turned more to a foreign policy agenda dedicated to issues involving the Cold War and the development of the European Union. By the mid-1980s, the responsibility for arranging the U.S.-EP meetings in the U.S. Congress and the formation of the congressional delegations to Europe shifted to the House Foreign Affairs Committee. As historic political events in Europe began to unfold in the late 1980s, the relevance and importance of the Congress–Parliament exchange began to increase under the leadership of former representatives Lee Hamilton, Tom Lantos, and Benjamin Gilman, who were strong supporters of close U.S.-European relations. These Members, along with a handful of others, focused on the implications of the end of the Cold War and the role the EU had the potential to play in the new European landscape; they all believed that Congress ought to try to better understand both the EU as a whole and its legislative process, a feeling that continues to be shared by many, although not all, even today.

Contacts between the U.S. Congress and the European Parliament have been stimulated from time to time by events that have contributed to the slow but steady evolution of ever-closer relations between the two institutions. Three such milestones include the creation of the Transatlantic Policy Network (TPN) in 1992; the launch of the New Transatlantic Agenda (NTA) in 1995; and the establishment of the Transatlantic Economic Council (TEC) in 2007.

Transatlantic Policy Network

The TPN was established in 1992 as a broad-based, multi-party group of EU and U.S. politicians, corporate leaders, influential think tank experts, and academics. It was (and remains) dedicated to encouraging constant dialogue and the maintenance of close personal relationships as a means to help both the United States and the EU identify their common interests and strengthen their partnership. The significance of the founding of TPN was that, for the first time, an outside organization provided a venue—apart from the semi-annual Congress-Parliament meetings—where Members and MEPs could study and debate specific issues, exchange views with an eye towards finding transatlantic solutions, and coordinate their actions with other U.S. government officials and EU policymakers.

New Transatlantic Agenda

Although the United States government and the European Union had been engaged in a political and economic partnership since 1954, the launch of the NTA in 1995 sought to provide a new framework intended to move the relationship essentially from one of consultation to one of joint action in several areas. Often overlooked in the statement outlining the goals and purposes of the NTA was the acknowledgment of the leaders of the United States and the EU that they "attached great importance to enhanced parliamentary links" and agreed to "consult with parliamentary leaders on both sides of the Atlantic regarding consultation mechanisms, including building on existing institutions, to discuss matters related to our transatlantic partnership."[5]

However, implementation of the provisions of the NTA was slow to develop. Even slower was implementation of the decision to consult with parliamentary leaders, in part because Congress and the European Parliament were uncertain on how to define the roles they might play in the NTA. In January 1999, after four years of little or no progress on incorporating the legislatures into a transatlantic decision-making process, and sensing a need to acknowledge the NTA's commitment to include the legislatures, the delegations of the U.S. House and the EP—at their 50th meeting—agreed to formalize the dialogue and to change the group's name to the Transatlantic Legislators' Dialogue (TLD). In announcing the formation of the TLD, the two delegations stated that the Dialogue "will constitute the formal response of the European Parliament and the U.S. Congress to the commitment in the New Transatlantic Agenda to enhance parliamentary ties between the European Union and the United States."[6] In response to the decision to re-name the interparliamentary exchange, the U.S. House in November 1999, during consideration of the Consolidated Appropriations Act for Fiscal Year 2000 (H.R. 3194/P.L. 106-113), amended Section 109(c) of the Department of State Authorization Act for Fiscal Years 1984/1985 (22 U.S.C. 276 note) to officially change the name of the group to the TLD.

Following the introduction of the NTA in 1995, a small minority of representatives in Congress and the European Parliament began arguing for greater legislative involvement in broader U.S.-EU relations, even including participation in the annual U.S.-EU Summit. The formal launch of the TLD provided new impetus for the kind of input these legislators hoped for, and efforts were made on both sides to reinforce the interests of the legislatures in assuming an enhanced role in the transatlantic relationship. Since the 1999 declaration officially establishing the TLD, numerous pieces of legislation have been introduced and even passed in both Congress and the Parliament expressing the importance of the transatlantic partnership, calling for enhanced dialogue and coordination between Congress and the EP, and asserting that the legislatures should be consulted more closely by U.S. and EU policymakers. In particular, related to the development of the transatlantic economic relationship outlined in the NTA, in 2004 and 2005, the EP and the U.S. House passed resolutions supporting, among other things, the completion of the transatlantic market by 2015. In 2006, the U.S. Senate passed a similar resolution.

Although those legislators dedicated to improving parliamentary input into the U.S.-EU relationship appeared prepared to take on a more substantive role, many observers note that the nature of transatlantic cooperation, the complexities of the issues, the multiple layers of agencies involved, the sometimes slow pace of reform, and the press of normal legislative business, have frequently hindered greater Congress-Parliament participation. To address some of these concerns on the U.S. side, the Chairman of the House International Relations Committee in 2000 created a new subcommittee solely dedicated to Europe. In 2005, several Members of the House agreed to establish a Members Caucus on the EU to consider the wide range of transatlantic political and economic issues. Both of these developments provided new venues for a more focused discussion of U.S.-EU relations among interested legislators. It was also hoped that the subcommittee and caucus would help the TLD to identify new Members with an interest in the EU and to assume a more active role in promoting transatlantic contact and cooperation.

In addition, since 1999 especially, organizations such as TPN, the German Marshall Fund of the United States, the Atlantic Council, the European Institute, and other public policy groups, have become more involved in developing and expanding the transatlantic knowledge-base of Congress and the European Parliament. Such groups hold briefings and host conferences on numerous U.S.-EU issues and promote international travel for Members and staff. Publications, such as the annual transatlantic economic report issued by the SAIS Center for Transatlantic Relations, have brought the importance of the economic dimension of the U.S.-EU partnership to the forefront and often highlight other specific elements of the relationship. All of these efforts have helped Members of Congress and the EP to better understand the nature of the transatlantic partnership, to identify issues of common interest, and to expand contacts and dialogue.

Transatlantic Economic Council

Despite the various measures described above to bolster ties between Congress and the European Parliament, the existence and purpose of the exchange between the U.S. House and the EP—at least on the U.S. side—continued to remain little known or understood, both within and outside the House. This appeared to be disappointing to some Members, MEPs, and other government officials and experts because over the previous decades, many congressional delegations had traveled to Europe and several senior Members of the House had participated in exchange activities or knew of the exchange sessions with the EP. For instance, in 1987, then-Speaker of the House Jim Wright attended the interparliamentary meeting in Madrid, and between 1994 and 2000, the Chairman of the House International Relations Committee also served as the U.S. Chair of the interparliamentary exchange with the EP.

However, some suggest that the creation of the TEC has helped elevate relations between the U.S. House and the EP perhaps more than any other previous initiative to strengthen the relationship. In January 2007, upon assuming the rotating six-month presidency of the EU, German Chancellor Angela Merkel proposed further liberalization of transatlantic trade and investment barriers by enhancing the existing cooperation among U.S. and EU regulatory agencies. In part, her proposal was in line with the provision in the New Transatlantic Agenda that called for the creation of a transatlantic marketplace by eliminating or reducing both tariff and non-tariff barriers that hindered the flow of goods, services, and capital between the United States and Europe. Building on the Merkel initiative, the April 2007 U.S.-EU Summit adopted a *Framework for Advancing Transatlantic Economic Integration*. The *Framework* affirmed the importance of further deepening transatlantic economic integration, particularly through efforts to reduce or harmonize regulatory barriers to international trade and investment. The TEC was established as a new institutional structure to advance the process of regulatory cooperation and barrier reduction by encouraging both U.S. and EU regulators to move forward on issues outlined in the *Framework*. It was agreed that the TEC would be headed on both sides by ministerial-level appointees with cabinet rank.

As part of its mandate, the TEC was directed to include a broader participation of stakeholders, including—for the first time in a formal regulatory framework—legislators. In particular, the *Framework* instructed the TEC to establish an "advisory group" that would draw upon the heads of the "existing transatlantic dialogues" to provide input and guidance on priorities for pursuing transatlantic economic integration. The existing transatlantic dialogues included the Transatlantic Business Dialogue (TABD), the Transatlantic Consumers Dialogue (TACD), and the Transatlantic Legislators' Dialogue (TLD).

The lack of knowledge about the TLD seemed to contribute to the surprise of many in the wider transatlantic community when the TEC leadership invited the TLD to be a member of its Advisory Group. In fact, it was unclear that anyone at the White House at the time of the 2007 U.S.-EU Summit contacted the House leadership to inform them a new role was to be asked of the legislative branch. Nor did it appear that anyone had informed the TLD Chairs that the TLD was to be handed a new and possibly far-reaching responsibility—that of formally representing the views of Congress and the European Parliament in the transatlantic economic integration and regulatory cooperation process.[7]

Nevertheless, many supporters of the effort to achieve a more barrier-free transatlantic marketplace believed that ultimate success could not be achieved without the strong commitment and active participation of the U.S. Congress and the European Parliament. Some advocates had long decried the low level of engagement by Congress and the Parliament in the overall economic integration and regulatory cooperation process. As such, proponents of giving the TLD a role in the TEC maintained that through more active oversight, legislators could articulate their support for, or concerns about, a particular regulatory direction before the regulators proceeded too far down the negotiation path. They also asserted that for the U.S. Congress, through its authorization and appropriation roles, Members could prod the regulators to move the cooperative efforts forward and provide the funds necessary to carry out that mandate. Finally, supporters noted that for the European Parliament, the implementation of the EU's new Lisbon Treaty would give the EP more decision-making authority over trade-related issues as well as an enlarged role in regulatory decision-making and oversight.

For those interested in the transatlantic economic relationship, the mandate to include the legislatures in the TEC process generated greater interest in the role that the U.S. Congress and the European Parliament can or should play in regulatory cooperation and convergence. This interest prompted immediate efforts by groups such as the Transatlantic Business Dialogue, the U.S. Chamber of Commerce, and the European-American Business Council, among others, to reach out to Congress and Parliament in order to inject more economic and regulatory specificity to the debate. Two recent reports, one co-authored by the Atlantic Council and the Bertelsmann Foundation,[8] and another co-authored by several U.S. and European think tanks entitled *Shoulder to Shoulder: Forging a Strategic U.S.-EU Partnership*,[9] have discussed the parameters that a regulatory cooperation dialogue should take, including how the transatlantic legislatures could play an influential role.

Some observers contend that the attempts by these outside organizations to increase awareness about transatlantic economic and regulatory issues, especially among some U.S. members and committees with relevant jurisdictions, *was* starting to have a some impact on both the narrow regulatory cooperation agenda as well as on the broader legislative relationship between the U.S. Congress and the European Parliament. Many of this view acknowledge that the transatlantic impact of legislation has rarely been a central consideration during the legislative process, whether in Congress or in the EP. Nor do they believe that Congress would submit its own legislative initiatives to any form of a transatlantic impact assessment or cede its authority to react to a national crisis, such as a terrorist attack or banking crisis, without first consulting the EU, or vice versa. However, some assert that efforts to improve congressional and EP understanding of the magnitude of the transatlantic economic relationship, and the increasing dialogue on transatlantic economic integration and regulatory cooperation, have helped to expand the U.S.-EU legislative partnership beyond the TEC-related issues and begun to result in a more notable desire by some in Congress to become more engaged with their counterparts in the EP.

THE CURRENT TRANSATLANTIC LEGISLATORS' DIALOGUE

Although the creation of the TEC and the appointment of the TLD to its Advisory Group perhaps did more to raise the visibility of the TLD than any other event over the past several years, the TLD remains relatively unknown in the U.S. Congress compared with its status in the European Parliament. Some suggest that a key reason for this disparity can be found in the structure and function of the TLD itself, which differs significantly between the U.S. Congress and the EP.

The European Parliament has a much more structured architecture for its participation in the TLD than does the U.S. Congress. At the start of each new

Parliament (the current one runs from 2009-2014), the EP adopts a resolution proposing a list of interparliamentary delegations and sets the number of MEPs that will constitute each delegation. At present, there are a total of 41 delegations in the Parliament.[10] The largest EP delegation is the Delegation for Relations with the United States (D-US), which currently consists of 53 MEPs. Each political group in the Parliament receives an allocation of delegation seats roughly proportional to its overall size in the EP. For example, the European People's Party (EPP), the largest political group in the EP, has 19 seats in the D-US whereas the Europe of Freedom and Democracy (EFD) group, which is the smallest in the EP, has 2 seats. Similarly, each political group receives an allocation of chairmanships/vice-chairs of the various delegations, with the largest group having the first choice of chair. In 2009, the EPP selected the chairmanship of the D-US as its first choice and named Elmar Brok, a German MEP, as Chair. MEPs are appointed to the delegation for the full five-year term of the Parliament. The D-US meets on a periodic basis to discuss a wide range of issues involving the transatlantic relationship as well as the upcoming TLD meetings.

In the EP, participants in the semi-annual TLD meetings are drawn from the D-US delegation. EP representation in the TLD (EUTLD) is led by a Steering Committee consisting of the Chairman and two Vice-Chairs of the D-US and ten MEPs who are the chairs of various EP standing committees ranging from International Trade to Environment, Public Health and Food Safety. The EUTLD Steering Committee is co-chaired by the Chairman of the D-US (Brok) and the Chairman of the Foreign Affairs Committee (Gabriele Albertini, an Italian MEP also in the EPP group), who lead the EUTLD delegation when it meets with its U.S. counterpart. The Steering Committee coordinates all activities of the TLD, ensures that there is broad representation of MEPs from the EP's committees at the TLD meetings, and reports to the D-US on its activities. The number of MEPs attending the annual TLD meetings is not limited and has often exceeded 20 members.

On the U.S. side, the Transatlantic Legislators' Dialogue is one of 13 Parliamentary and Commission Groups operating in Congress. Unlike some of the other exchanges, such as the NATO Parliamentary Assembly (NATOPA) or the British-American Parliamentary Group (BAPG), which also include the Senate, U.S. representation in the TLD (USTLD) is from the House only. In addition, the USTLD is not statutorily authorized, although it is authorized to receive funds each year to support its activities. Thus, while the NATOPA and the BAPG are authorized by statute to include a total of 24 official delegates (12 each from the House and Senate that are appointed by the Speaker of the

House and the Senate Majority Leader respectively), the TLD has no specified number of participants and no Speaker appointment.

Furthermore, official U.S. delegates of the statutorily authorized parliamentary exchanges are appointed for the duration of each Congress. The USTLD, by contrast, has no fixed term for its participants. Traditionally, the Chair and Ranking Member of the House Foreign Affairs Committee appointed the USTLD's Chair. In the 112th Congress it appears that the Chair (currently Representative Stearns, FL) was appointed by the Speaker, with the possible concurrence of the Chair of the Foreign Affairs Committee; the Vice-Chair (currently Representative Loretta Sanchez, CA) was appointed by the Minority Leader and the Ranking Member of the Foreign Affairs Committee. There is no formal nomination of any other USTLD delegate. Many Members have attended past meetings, but participation in the USTLD—at least until recently—often seemed to be on an ad hoc basis, with little continuity of participants and, in some instances, largely dependent on the ability of the USTLD Chair to convince members to attend the semi-annual meetings.[11] Moreover, the USTLD has no equivalent "Steering Committee". While some observers have suggested that the EU Caucus in the House serve as the umbrella organization from which TLD delegates could be drawn, there has been little association between the two, even though several Members of the House participate in both the Caucus and the TLD.

Although U.S. member participation in TLD sessions during the 111th Congress appeared to have reached a higher level of continuity, there is still concern among some observers that the TLD could continue to have difficulty attracting and maintaining a broad group of Members willing to participate on a regular basis. TLD supporters worry that the lack of sustained U.S. member participation hinders the development of personal relationships between legislators, seen as essential for a truly frank and open exchange of views and as necessary ultimately for greater legislative consultation and coordination. Similarly, while the EUTLD has representation from most of its key parliamentary committees, the USTLD is not structured to guarantee the inclusion of Members from all of the major congressional committees. Combined with the uncertainty over which Members will actually participate in the U.S. delegation each time the TLD meets, some MEPs have observed that the TLD sessions do not necessarily provide them with good U.S. contacts on matters of interest to them. Many in the transatlantic business and consumer communities—who are the TLD's partners in the TEC—also appear frustrated that there is no permanent list of USTLD delegates with whom they can meet on a regular basis to discuss issues related to the TEC and the regulatory agenda.[12]

Another difference between the U.S. Congress and the EP in relation to the TLD involves staffing. Traditionally, on the U.S. side, there have been three principal staff designated as the "U.S. secretariat" for the TLD: an administrator and one representative from the majority and minority. These staff are part of the House Foreign Affairs Committee structure and usually have large portfolios with many responsibilities beyond the TLD. Observers note that the Foreign Affairs Committee staff are highly professional, knowledgeable of transatlantic relations, and provide sufficient support for most security and foreign policy-related discussions at the TLD meetings. However, these same observers also point out that none of the key items on the U.S.-EU economic or regulatory agenda are ones that fall under the jurisdiction of the Foreign Affairs Committee.

In the view of many experts, it would likely be a real stretch to expect that Foreign Affairs Committee staff who are responsible for following issues and events in places ranging from Russia to Kosovo to Eurasia can somehow also find the time to become proficient on automobile crash testing, container scanning, toy safety, or hedge fund transparency. And, realistically, neither the Foreign Affairs Committee nor the USTLD Chair and Vice-Chairs could hire a whole cadre of staff with the kind of expertise needed to be responsive to the various issues under consideration by the TLD, particularly those in the TEC process. Although non-foreign policy matters are usually included in the TLD meeting agenda, it does not appear that there is regular contact between USTLD staff and other standing committee staff that would allow for coordination of issues and committee perspectives beyond foreign policy issues.

The EUTLD is also staffed by a secretariat, which includes six permanent EP staff dedicated to the coordination and operation of the TLD alone. Recently, the EUTLD secretariat has worked with the secretariats of the EP standing committees to designate a TLD Administrator for each committee; these Administrators are intended to act as interlocutors between the committees and the TLD, helping the TLD secretariat to identify issues that should be placed on the TLD meeting agenda and promoting greater coordination of views and positions. In the EP, the D-US falls under what is known as the Directorate-General for External Policy (DG-EXPO), which provides professional support for the EP committees on Foreign Affairs, Development, and International Trade, as well as for all of the EP delegations.

The DG-EXPO also includes a Policy Department whose staff provide research and background information for the delegations and committees, including the EUTLD.

INITIATIVES TO STRENGTHEN CONGRESS-PARLIAMENT COOPERATION

Since the launch of the TLD in 1999, there have been numerous calls on both sides of the Atlantic to find ways to develop even closer cooperation between Congress and the EP. Some in the European Parliament have gone so far as to suggest the creation of a transatlantic parliamentary assembly consisting of Members of Congress and the Parliament that would share joint responsibility for addressing issues of mutual interest through both oversight and legislative mechanisms. While this proposal has not found any support in the U.S. Congress, there have been two recent developments that have enhanced the opportunity for both legislatures to explore ways to work more directly with each other on selected issues.

European Parliament Liaison Office (EPLO)

As noted previously, although contact between Members of the U.S. House and the EP had taken place since 1972, some in the Parliament have been increasingly interested in developing relations with a broader audience in Congress. In 1984, then-EP President Klaus Haensch put forward a proposal in which he argued that it was important for MEPs to liaise directly with their counterparts in Congress, and suggested that the Parliament should have its own representation in Washington. This idea, in one form or another, has been part of the European Parliament's effort to establish "co-equality" with the U.S. Congress. However, it was only recently that the concept began to gain significant momentum. In 2006, MEP Elmar Brok, who was rapporteur for the EP's Committee on Foreign Affairs at the time, prepared a Parliament report on "improving EU-U.S. relations." Mr. Brok's report expressed a desire that the "EP budget for 2007 should establish a permanent post in Washington so that the Parliament and the Transatlantic Legislators' Dialogue (TLD) may maintain permanent contact with the U.S. House of Representatives and the Senate."

On March 26, 2009, the EP adopted a resolution on the state of transatlantic relations.[13] In that resolution, the Parliament restated a long-held view that the U.S. Congress and the EP should continue to develop a closer working relationship with respect to legislative initiatives in each other's institutions, should enhance cooperation between legislative committees, and should create a reciprocal "early-warning" system in order to identify potential legislative activities that could affect U.S.-EU relations. The resolution further "invited" the EP's Secretary-General to proceed as a "matter of utmost urgency" to implement a decision taken by the Parliament's Bureau on December 11, 2006, to open a parliamentary office in Washington and to deploy officials to serve as the EP's legislative liaison to the U.S. Congress, a responsibility that had up to that time been entrusted to the European Commission's Washington delegation.[14]

On April 29, 2010, Klaus Haensch's vision became a reality when EP President Jerzy Buzek officially opened the EPLO with the U.S. Congress in Washington and named Piotr Nowina-Konopka (former EP Director for Relations with National Parliaments) its first Director. Although the EPLO will develop contacts with a broad array of policymakers, think tanks, and other institutions in Washington, and will serve to facilitate visits by MEPs, the primary mission of the Liaison Office is to "build a network of Congress–Parliament staff who can work together on concrete issues requiring legislative and political cooperation or at least intellectual attention and understanding."[15] The EPLO will report directly to the EP Secretary-General. At the time of its opening, the Liaison Office had three professional and two administrative staff; by the middle of 2011, the EPLO had a total of 11 staff.

Interestingly, the 2009 EP resolution calling for the establishment of the EPLO also included language inviting the U.S. Congress to consider the possibility of setting up its own congressional liaison office in Brussels. The U.S. Congress, through periodic resolutions such as H.Res. 230 adopted in 2007, has long expressed support for closer cooperation between Congress and the EP. Some individual Members have endorsed practices such as instituting a legislative early warning system (often mentioned in the press releases issued at the end of TLD meetings), and a number of Members involved in the TLD appear to support the idea in principle of establishing a congressional liaison office in Brussels. At a December 15, 2009, hearing of the House Foreign Affairs Committee's Europe Subcommittee, the proposal for a Brussels office was raised and received a good deal of attention, including from the Subcommittee Chairman. To date, however, Congress as a whole has not demonstrated significant interest in or enthusiasm about establishing a reciprocal congressional liaison office in Brussels (for more information, see "Possible Options for Future Congress-Parliament Cooperation").

Closer Committee Contact[16]

Not long after the TLD was assigned an advisory role to the TEC, it became clear to some—including former MEP Jonathan Evans who served as Chair of the EUTLD from 2004 to 2009—that the structure of the TLD was not optimally organized to address the TLD's new responsibilities with respect to regulatory cooperation. Evans, along with some of his colleagues and a number of outside observers, felt that while most Members of Congress and the EP participating in the TLD were well versed to discuss a broad range of foreign policy issues at the TLD meetings, the same could not necessarily be said when it came to talking about more technical regulatory matters. Given the wide array of issues in the regulatory dialogue—including the mutual recognition of accounting standards, supply chain security, copyright and patent protection, preferred traveler programs, cosmetics testing, and medical device certification—an unstructured TLD might find itself further down the learning curve than its transatlantic business and consumer partners in the TEC, thus requiring TLD delegates to spend time catching up on such issues. This, in turn, could present a problem for some TLD participants who might be reluctant to become more specialized in economic and regulatory matters at the expense of other broader transatlantic policy issues. Moreover, such participants would probably not want the TLD to become strictly TEC-issue oriented. As a result, Evans suggested that Congress and the Parliament consider ways to improve direct committee-to-committee contact on specific issues and for the TLD to develop mechanisms whereby it could tap the expertise of the committees and their staffs when necessary for the TLD meetings or for the TLD response to the TEC.

Like U.S. congressional committees, EP committees are key actors in the adoption of EU legislation. Currently, the EP has 20 standing committees and 2 "special" committees, which investigate or oversee specific issues for a limited period of time. In the U.S. Congress, the House and Senate have similar lists of standing committees, albeit not exactly the same. Committee jurisdictions are defined by the rules of each chamber and the House and Senate committee jurisdictions are not always parallel. For example, the

Senate Agriculture Committee is responsible for child nutrition legislation, whereas that responsibility is handled in the House by the House Education and Workforce Committee (and not the House Agriculture Committee).

Unlike the U.S. Congress, each EP committee has a chairman and four vice-chairmen. The political make-up of the EP committees reflects that of the Parliament as a whole and committee posts are allocated proportional to the respective size of the political groups; for example, the largest group (the EPP) currently chairs nine committees, the second-largest group (the S&D) seven, and the third-largest group (the ALDE) three. Committee activity is a process of coordination among the chair and vice-chairs. In the U.S. House and Senate, all committees are chaired by a member of the majority party and although the minority is often consulted on committee activity, the committee's authority is centered in its chair. In practice, a chair's prerogative includes determining the committee's agenda, deciding when to take or delay action, presiding during meetings, and controlling most funds allocated by the chamber to the committee.

Because of the high volume and complexity of its work, Congress divides its legislative, oversight, and internal administrative tasks among committees and subcommittees. Committees and subcommittees gather information; compare and evaluate legislative alternatives; identify policy problems and propose solutions to them; select, determine the text of, and report out measures for the full chambers to consider; monitor executive branch performance (oversight); and conduct investigations. Subcommittees only have the power and authority granted to them by the full committee. For example, some subcommittees hold hearings, but do not consider legislation. Subcommittees and their areas of responsibility may also change from one Congress to the next. Furthermore, subcommittees cannot report bills directly to the floor. In the Parliament, the work of the committees is much the same, but only one committee—the Foreign Affairs Committee—has subcommittees.

A significant difference between Congress and the EP, however, is the way legislation is handled. In the U.S. Congress, legislation may be introduced by any Member of Congress. In the House, the legislation is referred to a committee based on "primary" jurisdiction. Measures can also be sequentially referred to additional committees, and many measures are referred to more than one panel. In the Senate, measures are referred based on "predominant" jurisdiction and it is rare for measures to be referred to more than one committee.

In the European Union, as noted previously, legislation is first proposed by the European Commission and then submitted to the Parliament and the Council of Ministers. The EP and the Council share legislative authority in most policy areas and must both approve a Commission proposal for it to become EU law. All EU legislation must have its legal basis in the EU treaties (upon which the EU has been built) or in a piece of secondary legislation, and each legislative proposal must cite in its preamble the EU treaty article upon which it is based. (Interestingly, a new rule adopted by the Republican leadership for the 112th Congress would require that all bills introduced should provide the "constitutional authority" for their provisions.) The legal basis determines which committee is deemed the "competent" committee to consider the legislative proposal, as well as the procedure under which the legislation is considered, (i.e., whether the Parliament has the benefit of the "ordinary legislative procedure" (co-decision) whereby it decides jointly with the Council on a proposal presented by the Commission).[17] Under Parliament's rules of procedure, if the designated competent committee wishes to challenge the legal basis of a piece of proposed legislation, it must consult the Legal Affairs Committee.

Once legislation is submitted to the competent committee, the EP committee appoints an MEP as "rapporteur" to draft a report on the legislation under consideration. The rapporteur submits a draft report to the committee for discussion, and the committee votes on and possibly amends the report. This is similar to a congressional committee mark-up of legislation. The committee's report is then considered in a plenary session of the entire Parliament (similar to how legislation is considered by the whole House or Senate), amended if necessary, and put to a vote in the full EP. The Parliament thus adopts its position on the proposed EU legislation.

Observers suggest that differences between the two bodies' legislative processes are a key issue when considering whether the U.S. Congress and the EP can effectively work with each other on matters of common interest that might involve legislation. Given that the European Commission is the originator of EU legislation, coordinating the legislative process between the two legislatures could be difficult especially because the U.S. Congress can introduce legislation and consider it as rapidly or as deliberately as it wishes. To have legislation run parallel in both legislatures, the Commission would probably have to submit a legislative proposal around the same time a similar piece was introduced in either the House or Senate. Although the EP can ask the Commission to introduce legislation on a particular issue that might be under consideration in Congress and that the Parliament believes should be addressed, the Commission can take up to six months to decide whether or not it will submit legislation in response to the EP's request. Even if the Commission decided to comply, the process of developing the actual legislative proposal could take up to one year or longer. Thus, it would require much coordination to have legislation considered on a simultaneous or near-simultaneous basis in both Congress and the EP, as well as a strong political commitment from both sides to do so.

Analysts also note that there are some issues in which the Parliament may have a legislative say, but Congress does not, and vice-versa. For example, when the renewal of the U.S.-EU SWIFT agreement was considered, the Parliament played a key role and rejected the accord initially. Later, after changes were negotiated between the European Commission and the U.S. government, the Parliament held a second vote and approved the agreement. During this whole process, the SWIFT accord was not sent to the U.S. Congress for consideration because it was negotiated by the United States as an executive agreement. Similarly, with the previously mentioned U.S.-EU PNR agreement, the EP will have a legislative role in approving any revised agreement. However, while both Houses of Congress have introduced resolutions expressing concern with any potential changes to the existing agreement, it is not expected to come before Congress for approval; it is a U.S. executive agreement and most experts believe it is unlikely that the Obama Administration would agree to any EU demands that would necessitate changes to U.S. laws. Given such differences between the U.S. and EU policymaking processes, some skeptics question whether stronger Congressional-EP relations would add much value. Others contend, however, that even in matters such as the former SWIFT or the current PNR issue—in which one side has a legislative role and the other does not—closer ties and personal relationships between Members of Congress and their counterparts in the EP could help sway the debate and perhaps produce more favorable outcomes.

Despite some differences in the way legislation is handled in Congress and the EP, many experts assert that there appears to be opportunities for committees in both bodies to track what issues are being considered and where interests intersect. Possible mechanisms for doing so include video conferences, joint hearings, delegation visits, and staff exchanges. As mentioned, the EP has already identified "TLD administrators" for each EP committee; in addition to informing the TLD of what issues are under consideration in the committees, it is hoped that these administrators will also become points-of-contact for their counterpart committee staff in Congress.

For a comparison of European Parliament committees and House and Senate committees with similar or related jurisdictions, see the Appendix.

POSSIBLE OPTIONS FOR FUTURE CONGRESS-PARLIAMENT COOPERATION

As the level of contact between the U.S. Congress and the European Parliament has increased and as more observers begin to advocate for closer cooperation between the two bodies, several ideas have been put forward to help strengthen the overall effectiveness of the Congress-to-Parliament partnership. While the European Parliament has been far out in front of Congress in the pursuit of a stronger relationship, as noted earlier, the U.S. Congress as a whole has not seemed to embrace the need for significantly closer ties. Nevertheless, should Congress deem it worthwhile in the months or years ahead to further develop relations with the EP, there are a number of potential options that could be considered and explored.

Seven possible options for enhancing Congress-Parliament cooperation are discussed below; several focus on the TLD, some are specific to the USTLD, and others pertain to the broader Congress-EP relationship. Some observers suggest that a new structure on the U.S. side is needed to oversee and guide Congress-EP relations. However, others contend that appropriate structures already exist to do this; the U.S. Congress and its committees and subcommittees, the EU Caucus, and the TLD itself provide the necessary structure for managing the Congress-EP relationship. For those of this view, the issue is not necessarily to create a new structure but to try to make the existing structure work more effectively.

1. Enhance the Transatlantic Legislators' Dialogue

For some, the first step in any attempt to boost Congress-EP relations and enhance the effectiveness of the TLD might be to elevate the status of the USTLD by having the TLD formally authorized by statute. Short of that, supporters of this option have suggested that Members of the House could be appointed to the TLD by the Speaker for the full two years of a Congress and the number of U.S. delegates to the TLD could be firmly established (e.g., at 12, with up to eight additional delegation seats open to any Member interested). In appointing Members to the TLD, it has been suggested that the Speaker should ensure representation from a cross-section of standing committees in the House. The proposed list of candidates could be developed through a consultation process between the Chair/Vice-Chairs of the USTLD and the chairs of the standing committees. It appears that for the 112th Congress, the Speaker notified the Chair of the USTLD of his appointment, but as of June 2011 it does not appear that additional members of the TLD had been appointed by anyone.

Some proponents of this option believe that the Congressional Caucus on the EU should be revitalized and form the umbrella organization for Congress-EP relations, much like the EP's Delegation for Relations with the United States. As discussed more below, the EU Caucus could also be open to the U.S. Senate. Some observers suggest that it might be beneficial for the appointed USTLD delegates to become the core of the EU Caucus; other members of the Caucus could act as substitutes for any USTLD delegate unable to attend a particular session or serve as additional USTLD participants.

Some advocates of enhancing the TLD have also proposed that in appointing the TLD Chair, the Speaker or Chair of the Foreign Affairs Committee also identify a few specific issues that the TLD should focus on and that the USTLD Chair, in conjunction with the EUTLD should establish either political and economic committees within which those issues would be addressed, or specific working groups to focus on those issues. TLD Chair Stearns, in a recent press release, noted three major issues for the TLD to address: cross-border security and visa and cargo harmonization; financial services and improving financial stability; and agriculture, specifically food safety and genetically modified organisms. Should the TLD decide in the future to set up either committees or working groups, some have suggested that in addition to assigning U.S. and European TLD members as chairs and vice-chairs, rapporteurs might also be assigned to research and report on specific issues. Supporters assert that this structure would offer Members and MEPs the opportunity to focus more sustained attention on issues in which they may have a particular interest or expertise. The TLD committee or working group chairs would report on the topics discussed in their committees to the entire body at some point during the TLD meetings. Another suggestion would be for the TLD to be more active in between its semi-annual meetings by promoting on-going dialogue between committee chairs, rapporteurs, and other delegates through the use of video conferences so that TLD members can keep in touch year-round.

Some observers have also argued that it may be worth considering hiring one or two dedicated USTLD staff in the House, instead of relying on the current structure of utilizing Foreign Affairs Committee staff. These permanent USTLD staff could potentially become part of the Speaker's Office of Interparliamentary Affairs. Such permanent USTLD staff could coordinate the activities of the TLD, help the USTLD liaise with standing committee staff, and meet regularly with representatives of the EP's Washington liaison office. In addition, the USTLD might consider establishing its own website to keep Members informed of its activities.

Pros and Cons. Supporters of enhancing the existing TLD—especially by having it authorized in statute in the U.S. Congress and having the Speaker officially appoint U.S. delegates—maintain that such measures would raise the standing of the TLD in the House and guarantee a more consistent group of attendees, especially on the U.S. side. Assigning Members and MEPs as chairs, vice-chairs, and rapporteurs of the proposed TLD committees could also convey a sense of "ownership" within the TLD and hopefully generate more dialogue in between the semi-annual TLD meetings. In addition, advocates assert that establishing TLD committee rapporteurs to report on specific issues might increase liaison between the TLD and the standing committees given that the rapporteurs would most likely contact the respective standing committees in their own institutions to discuss their research efforts. The research projects undertaken by the rapporteurs would also provide the opportunity for TLD staff to be in contact with each other on a more regular basis and with appropriate committee staff; as a result, TLD staff would be better able to help identify key issues on which both institutions may be working and where the potential may exist to pursue parallel tracks on legislation.

Skeptics of this option contend, however, that it would require a significant amount of political will in both bodies—but especially in the U.S. Congress—for it to materialize. In particular, they argue, this option would likely require a strong commitment not only from those Members currently involved in the TLD but also from the Speaker, in order to sufficiently convey to Members the importance of participating in this interparliamentary group.
Those of this view also doubt that the House leadership would be receptive to hiring additional staff dedicated to the TLD given the current political and economic climate.

2. Develop Closer TLD Coordination with the Standing Committees and Promote Committee Cooperation

As noted previously, one problem that has arisen since the launch of the TLD in 1999 is that no single committee—in either Congress or the EP—exercises jurisdiction over the broad array of issues on the transatlantic agenda, and particularly now on the regulatory agenda. In the U.S. House, the committee that has the primary authority to oversee the transatlantic political relationship—the Foreign Affairs Committee under House Rule X—has no authority on the specific regulatory issues under consideration by the TEC. And while the close connection between the USTLD and the Foreign Affairs Committee continues, it remains unclear whether other House committees—such as Financial Services, Judiciary, or Homeland Security—would necessarily defer to the TLD to provide advice and guidance to the TEC on issues that fall within their jurisdictions, such as accounting standards, technology innovation, intellectual property, and border control measures.

Thus, many observers argue that an information-sharing process must be established between the TLD and the standing committees, especially on the U.S. side. As mentioned above, the European Parliament has already sought to address the TLD-committee relationship in two ways. First, the EUTLD requires representation from most of the EP's standing committees. Second, each EP committee has identified a "TLD Administrator" on its staff to act as the liaison between the committee and the TLD, and at some point, between the committee and its counterpart committee in Congress. Any such TLD-to-committee interaction in the U.S. Congress seems to occur, at best, on an ad hoc basis.

In addition to promoting closer links between the TLD and the standing committees in each legislature, some experts suggest that the committees themselves should explore ways to work directly and more closely with each other (on the U.S. side, some contend both House and Senate committees should be involved). In part, this could be accomplished through video conferences, joint hearings, and delegation visits. One example of where this cooperation might work is in the agriculture sector. The 112th Congress has begun the process to reauthorize the U.S. farm bill over the next two years. At the same time, the EU's Common Agriculture Policy is up for renewal in 2012. Since agricultural policy, farm and export subsidies, and phytosanitary issues are politically important on both sides of the Atlantic, the U.S. and EP agriculture committees could explore how they could work in concert with each other. Here, the EU Caucus and the TLD could play a substantive role in helping coordinate the interaction between Committees as well as sponsoring workshops and briefings for all Member of Congress and EP on the issues involved in the Farm Bill/CAP debate. As noted above, TLD Chair Cliff Stearns has identified agriculture as a major upcoming issue for the TLD.

Pros and Cons. Proponents of developing better ties between the TLD and the standing committees stress that for at least the TEC responsibilities of the TLD, it is essential that committees with jurisdiction over issues on the TEC agenda be included in the TLD dialogue in some way. They assert that this is necessary because when the TEC meets and issues its recommendations on how the United States and EU might deal with matters such as consumer product safety or port security functions, it likely does so with what it believes to be the best guidance from the House of Representatives and the Parliament as a whole, not just from two or three individual Members of Congress or the EP who happen to be the TLD Chairs and Vice-Chairs. In addition, supporters contend that strengthening coordination between the TLD and the standing committees would allow for greater committee input into what should be included on the TLD meeting agendas and could help bring more U.S. members with relevant expertise into the dialogue with the European Parliament.

Some observers point out, however, that developing closer TLD coordination with the standing committees on the U.S. side would likely take some time and would require a sustained effort by the USTLD Chair. Given the still limited knowledge about the TLD and the EP in Congress, many committees would have to be convinced as to why cooperation might be in their interests. In terms of establishing direct committee-to-committee contact in an effort to improve legislative coordination between the two sides, others argue that some U.S. members might also be hesitant to pursue this option for fear of being seen as putting the interests of the transatlantic relationship ahead of those of their own constituents.

3. Utilize European Parliament Liaison Staff Deployed to Washington

This option would take advantage of the Parliament's decision to deploy its own liaison staff to Washington. Under this option, regular meeting or briefings between the EPLO and the USTLD chairs, USTLD delegates, the EU Caucus, and staff could be arranged to share insights, observations, and other information regarding activities in both Congress and the EP. As EP staffers are already in Washington and have a direct line of communication back to the Parliament, they would presumably be able to update Members and staff on legislative proposals under consideration in the EP.

Pros and Cons. Supporters of this option note that it could likely be implemented quickly given that the staff of the EPLO appear eager to establish good, close relations with Members of Congress and their staffs and would likely welcome the opportunity to have a regular exchange of views. For many U.S. Members and staffers, this option would also have the advantage of being relatively low-cost in terms of both money and time, but could help promote more dialogue among TLD delegates in between the semi-annual meetings. Others argue that this option may not be sufficient to significantly bolster the Congress-Parliament relationship. Some also question whether this option could be structured enough to bring into the TLD dialogue a broader range of committee staff on a regular and sustained basis.

4. Establish a Senior Staff "Fellowship" Exchange

Under this option, senior congressional staffers from either the Leadership offices or standing committees could be designated by the House and/or Senate Leadership as congressional "fellows" and seconded to the EP for a short-duration rotation (perhaps 2-3 months) with possibly the EP Secretariat, a selected EP committee, or the EP's Unit for Transatlantic Relations. This kind of exchange could accommodate up to 3 or 4 staff rotating to Brussels over the course of a year and would provide staff exposure to the Parliament as well as an avenue for continuous information exchange. Issues such as housing and other per diem costs would have to be determined by Congress but under a "fellowship" type of program, it would appear that congressional staff could hold an office and use equipment provided by the EP within the EP itself, much as foreign "fellows" can work out of congressional offices.

Pros and Cons. Advocates of establishing a fellowship exchange assert that this option would have the possible benefit of creating a cadre of U.S. staffers with first-hand knowledge of the EP and how it functions, as well as personal contacts within the EP. This could help further the goal of developing closer links between Congress and the EP. On the negative side, some point out that rotating U.S. congressional staff through Brussels on a short-term basis might not allow for the time necessary to establish strong relationships with EP counterparts that could prove sustainable and useful in the future. Others note that many congressional staffers—even at the senior level—often rotate in and out of congressional service, potentially limiting the utility of such a fellowship program in terms of enhancing institutional ties between Congress and the EP.

5. Utilize the Current Staff Employed by the U.S. Mission to the EU in Brussels

Currently, the U.S. Mission to the EU in Brussels, Belgium, employs staff to help follow the activities of the European Parliament. The staff track the work of the EP and submit reports to the Mission and the State Department. Some observers have suggested that it may be possible for the House Leadership to arrange with the State Department to have these individuals also send their reports to either the Leadership office or the TLD staff. Details of the exact responsibilities and reporting requirements of the U.S. Mission staff to Congress would have to be clearly defined; one key question would be whether the U.S. Mission staff could be "tasked" with specific requests from Members of Congress or staff about EP activities and legislation. In addition, Congress and the State Department would have to work out the security arrangements for the transfer of reports and other materials in a timely manner from the Mission to Congress.

Pros and Cons. Supporters of this option point out that it could provide Members of Congress and staffers with greater insights into the work of the EP and potentially enable Congress and the TLD to keep better track of legislative proposals under consideration in the EP, especially those that could affect U.S. interests. On the downside, some note that the State Department and the U.S. Mission to the EU might be neither willing nor able to accommodate such a congressional request for a variety of legal, financial, and security reasons. This option could also raise the question of the Executive/Legislative relationship and some contend that it could run the risk of Mission censorship of the information being provided to Congress.

6. Deploy Congressional Staff to Brussels

This option, similar to what the EP has already done, would involve opening a congressional liaison office in Brussels and deploying U.S. congressional staff there to work with the European Parliament on a daily basis. Aside from the logistical issues of work visas, diplomatic status, per diem, and others, this option would raise a series of questions for Congress such as who hires the employees, who do they report to (the Speaker and/or Senate Majority Leader, Committees, TLD leadership), and how does the minority party fit in. Other issues for consideration would include whether U.S. congressional staff could legally occupy office space inside the Parliament and whether Congress would pay rent and operating costs to the Parliament. As a variation of this option, some observers have suggested that it might be possible for congressional staff to work out of the U.S. Mission to the EU, much as the EPLO has been established administratively within the office space of the Washington Delegation of the European Union.

Pros and Cons. Proponents of this option assert that establishing a congressional liaison office in Brussels would be one of the most effective ways to pursue greater legislative consultation and cooperation between Congress and the EP. U.S. staffers deployed to Brussels would be able to follow events in the Parliament closely and keep U.S. Members, committees, and congressional staff informed of EP views and activities on a regular basis. Congressional staff in Brussels would also be well placed to develop working relationships with MEPs, EP committees, and EP staffers; in turn, they could connect Members and MEPs with similar legislative interests and help promote greater dialogue on key issues.

Critics contend, however, that establishing a congressional liaison office in Brussels is premature. In the absence of a broader political commitment from the U.S. Congress to boost ties with the EP, it appears difficult to even bolster the TLD let alone establish a whole new congressional entity focused on the EP. Although some of this view acknowledge that the EP's new liaison office in Washington may help develop closer relations between the EP and Congress, they assert that most Members of Congress are not convinced of the need to coordinate legislation with the EP or to have a reciprocal presence in Brussels at this time. Establishing a congressional liaison office in Brussels would also be a considerable logistical undertaking and depending on the eventual size of the office and the specific staff and housing arrangements, could entail a significant financial expenditure. Some observers worry that a congressional liaison office in Brussels could also set a precedent and lead to unrealistic expectations that Congress might seek to establish similar offices in other countries. Possibly locating congressional staff within the U.S. Mission to the EU would likely require extensive negotiations with the U.S. State Department and could raise constitutional questions about the separation of powers.

7. Establish a Congressional Commission on the EU

Some proponents of forging closer ties between Congress and the EP have called for establishing a Congressional Commission on the EU to monitor relevant EU legislation, evaluate its implications for the United States, and serve as the primary congressional liaison with the EP and the other EU institutions. Supporters of such an initiative assert that it could be largely modeled on the existing U.S. Helsinki Commission, an independent government agency, which since 1976 has sought to encourage compliance with the political commitments made by the member states of the Organization for Security and Cooperation in Europe (OSCE). Like the Helsinki Commission, it has been suggested that a Congressional Commission on the EU should include an equal number of Members from both the House and Senate, and representatives from both the majority and minority; the Commission's chair and vice-chair would rotate each new Congress between the House and Senate. The Commission would be able to hold hearings and meetings on matters of mutual interest to Congress and the EP.

In January 2011, H.Con.Res. 2 was introduced (Representative Issa, CA) proposing the creation of such a Commission along the lines described above. Although most of the staff of this potential Commission would presumably be located in Washington, H.Con.Res. 2 also allows for the provision of funds for the lease of office space by the Commission at or near the EP in Brussels.

Pros and Cons. Advocates of establishing a Congressional Commission on the EU argue that it would likely focus greater attention on the Congress-EP relationship and the U.S.-EU partnership more broadly, although some point out that it is unclear how a Commission could be any more effective than the Europe Subcommittees, the EU Caucus, or the TLD in raising awareness of the EU. As proposed in H.Con.Res. 2, a primary purpose of the Commission would be to monitor and assess EU legislation and its potential impact on the United States; in doing so, some suggest it could help to strengthen the TLD by demonstrating the EP's growing influence and the importance of increasing congressional engagement with the EP. In appointing Members to serve on the Commission, it would create a small but invested group of Members with a sustained interest in the EU and the EP. Proponents also point out that it would bring the Senate formally into the growing dialogue with the EP. And as a liaison between Congress and the EP, such a Commission could help to improve committee-to-committee relations between the two bodies and/or provide an "early warning" mechanism for legislation under consideration in either the EP or Congress.

On the other hand, critics assert that this option is also premature given the lack of wider congressional interest in promoting closer cooperation with the EP at this time. They also argue that there is nothing in the proposal for a new Commission that could not already be done under the current structures, and that the creation of a such a Commission would not necessarily guarantee a more effective or productive Congress-Parliament relationship. Some analysts point out that it is unclear how the proposed Commission would relate to the TLD, or whether a TLD would even be required, and they question whether the Senate would be willing or interested in participating (see below). Others believe that if the current TLD were enhanced and if the standing committees in both the U.S. Congress and the EP were to increase direct contact with each other, such a Commission would be redundant. Moreover, amid the current U.S. political climate, some doubt that the proposed Commission could garner the necessary support in the near future, in part because it would likely entail additional financial and staffing commitments.

ROLE OF THE SENATE

Many observers have raised the question of what role the Senate might play in efforts to strengthen ties between the U.S. Congress and the European Parliament. For the operation of the TLD in general, the Senate has never been involved. Visiting EP delegations coming to the United States for TLD meetings or for consultations with Members of Congress have paid courtesy calls occasionally on the Senate but the Senate has never participated formally in the TLD sessions. Recently, Senator Shaheen, Chair of the Europe Subcommittee of the Senate Foreign Relations Committee, has indicated her interest and intent in exploring ways the Senate could be involved with the TLD although there has been no intent to create a Senate version of the TLD or to statutorily establish a TLD with both House and Senate participation up to this point. Some observers believe that a reinvigorated House EU Caucus could reach out to the Senate to include some Senators as Members of the Caucus, thus giving the Senate contact with the activities of the TLD. Others believe that interested Senators should consider creating a Senate EU Caucus and then offer to hold joint meetings/briefings with the House counterpart. Through a joint Caucus effort, the Senate could potentially participate in TLD meetings as additional USTLD delegates (as described above in Option 1).

For many experts, the fact that the Senate has a co-equal role in regulatory oversight, but is not included as part of the TLD for purposes of the TEC Advisory Group, is a serious concern. As of December 2010, the TEC had met five times with the Advisory Group, yet there does not seem to be a formal mechanism within the TLD to include the Senate in its discussions with the TEC nor is there a way within the TEC Advisory Group to solicit Senate opinion. Thus, while the TLD over time could develop some level of authority to represent the views of the House on issues addressed in the Advisory Group's meetings with the TEC, the TLD, as currently structured, cannot claim to speak on behalf of the Senate. Many observers assert that this oversight must be addressed if the TEC intends to receive the advice of the whole Congress.

One option that would allow the TLD to continue its broad mandate to address a wide range of transatlantic issues and at the same time include the Senate in its role as a TEC advisor, may be for the USTLD Chair to consider creating a Congressional TEC Working Group. This Working Group would include Members from both the House and Senate who sit on committees with jurisdiction over issues on the TEC Advisory Group meeting agenda in order to encourage Senate input into the TEC process. At a December 2009 hearing of the Senate Foreign Relations Committee's Europe Subcommittee, the issue of the TLD and the role of the Senate in the TEC process was addressed by the witnesses and, according to Committee staff, will apparently be investigated further.

Some observers suggest that any efforts to elevate the broader Congress-Parliament relationship must have Senate participation. For example, Senate committees might also be encouraged to establish direct contact with EP committees with similar jurisdictions. As noted previously, while Senator Shaheen has raised the issue, it remains unclear to what extent Members of the Senate may be interested in developing relations with the EP, establishing ties with MEPs, or forging closer links between the relevant Senate and EP committees.

CONCLUSION

The European Parliament places a premium on its partnership with the U.S. Congress, and is committed to developing closer relations between the two legislative bodies. As noted above, the EP has implemented its long-held intention to open a legislative liaison office in Washington to increase its presence in Congress. And in recognition of the wide array of legislative issues facing Congress and the EP that could affect the broader transatlantic relationship, the EP has sought to involve its various standing committees in the work of the TLD in an attempt to enhance its effectiveness and utility.

On the U.S. side, however, Congress—other than those Members who have participated in the TLD—does not seem to be, at least at this point, as interested as the European Parliament in trying to establish closer legislative cooperation. Some attribute this lack of enthusiasm on the U.S. side to the fact that many believe that the two institutions do not have the exact same legislative powers or mandates. And many Members of Congress believe that the TLD, although never intended to be anything more than a mechanism for exchanging views among parliamentarians, currently welds little influence or authority as a transatlantic policy resource.

Nevertheless, the involvement of the TLD in the TEC's efforts to move regulatory cooperation toward the ultimate goal of an unencumbered transatlantic marketplace has raised the TLD's visibility in the U.S. Congress. It has also brought to light several questions about the role that Congress and the EP will or should play not only in the promotion of greater transatlantic economic integration and regulatory cooperation, but also how the two institutions might help shape the broader U.S.-EU relationship. Given the EP's growing power and influence within the EU as a result of the Lisbon Treaty, some U.S. officials and Members of Congress believe that it may be in U.S. interests for Congress to develop closer ties with the Parliament.

Many experts believe that if the identified concerns about the TLD are more fully addressed, the TLD could become an organization capable of taking on a more important stakeholder role in promoting Congress-Parliament cooperation and a stronger voice for transatlantic relations in both Congress and the EP. In the near term, however, these analysts acknowledge that the TLD's most immediate challenge will remain fulfilling its responsibilities as a member of the TEC Advisory Group. In the longer term, most observers stress that significantly bolstering the overall relationship between Congress and the

Parliament will require a sustained political commitment on both sides and serious consideration of all possible options, including but not necessarily limited to those focused on the TLD.

APPENDIX. COMPARISON OF COMMITTEES IN THE EUROPEAN PARLIAMENT AND THE U.S. CONGRESS

The following chart identifies the European Parliament (EP) committees and the U.S. House and Senate committees with similar or related jurisdictions. However, due to the unique nature of both systems, not all EP committees have a corresponding congressional equivalent. For organizational purposes, committees are grouped into broad "subject areas" given the various competencies of both EP and U.S. committees. These "subject areas" have been generally determined by EP committee competencies; accordingly, not all U.S. congressional committees are included.

Given the complexities of the U.S. committee system in particular, this chart is meant largely for illustrative purposes, and should not be construed as an exhaustive treatment of committee jurisdictions or competencies. Both EP and U.S. congressional committees are listed in alphabetical order.

Table A-1. Comparison of Committees in the EP and the U.S. Congress

Subject Area	EP Committees	Related U.S. Congressional Committees	
		House	Senate
Foreign Affairs and International Development	• Development • Foreign Affairs	• Armed Services • Foreign Affairs	• Armed Services • Foreign Relations
International Trade	• International Trade	• Ways and Means	• Finance
Budget and Appropriation Issues	• Budgetary Control • Budgets • Policy Challenges[a]	• Appropriations • Budget	• Appropriations • Budget
Economic and Monetary Policies	• Economic and Monetary Affairs • Financial, Economic and Social Crisis[a] • Internal Market and Consumer Protection	• Financial Services • Judiciary • Ways and Means	• Banking, Housing, and Urban Affairs • Finance • Judiciary
		• Joint House & Senate Economic Committee	

Table A-1. (Continued)

Subject Area	EP Committees	Related U.S. Congressional Committees	
		House	Senate
Social, Environmental, and Natural Resource Issues	• Culture and Education • Employment and Social Affairs	• Agriculture • Education and the Workforce	• Agriculture, Nutrition and Forestry • Commerce, Science, and Transportation
	• Environment, Public Health, and Food Safety • Women's Rights and Gender Equality	• Energy and Commerce • Judiciary • Science, Space and Technology • Small Business • Ways and Means	• Energy and Natural Resources • Environment and Public Works • Finance • Health, Education, Labor and Pensions • Judiciary • Small Business and Entrepreneurship
Technology, Infrastructure, and Transportation	• Industry, Research and Energy • Transport and Tourism	• Energy and Commerce • Science, Space, and Technology • Transportation and Infrastructure	• Commerce, Science and Transportation • Energy and Natural Resources • Environment and Public • Works
Agriculture, Fisheries, and Regional Development	• Agriculture and Rural Development • Fisheries • Regional Development	• Agriculture • Energy and Commerce • Natural Resources • Small Business	• Agriculture, Nutrition, and Forestry • Commerce, Science, and Transportation • Energy and Natural Resources • Environment and Public Works • Small Business and Entrepreneurship
Homeland Security and Civil Liberties	• Civil Liberties, Justice, and Home Affairs	• Homeland Security • Judiciary • Permanent Select Committee on Intelligence	• Homeland Security and Governmental Affairs • Judiciary • Select Committee on Intelligence
Legal and Constitutional Issues	• Legal Affairs • Constitutional Affairs	• Judiciary	• Judiciary
Other	• Petitions	• No equivalent	• No equivalent

Source: This chart was prepared by Kristin Archick, Specialist in European Affairs, Foreign Affairs, Defense and Trade Division, and Judy Schneider, Specialist on the Congress, Government and Finance Division, CRS.

a. Temporary EP Committee.

End Notes

[1] The current 27 members of the EU are: Austria, Belgium, Bulgaria, Cyprus, the Czech Republic, Denmark, Estonia, Finland, France, Germany, Greece, Hungary, Ireland, Italy, Latvia, Lithuania, Luxembourg, Malta, the Netherlands, Poland, Portugal, Romania, Slovakia, Slovenia, Spain, Sweden, and the United Kingdom.

[2] Daniel S. Hamilton and Joseph P. Quinlan, *The Transatlantic Economy 2011*, Center for Transatlantic Relations, 2011.

[3] The Lisbon Treaty seeks to reform the EU's governing institutions and decision-making processes in order to enable an enlarged Union to function more effectively. In addition to implementing a number of changes in how the EP and the other EU institutions operate, the Lisbon Treaty seeks to give the EU a stronger and more coherent voice on the world stage and to increase democratic transparency within the EU. For more information, see CRS Report RS21618, *The European Union's Reform Process: The Lisbon Treaty*, by Kristin Archick and Derek E. Mix.

[4] U.S. Ambassador to the European Union William E. Kennard, "Improving Relations Between the U.S. Congress and the European Parliament: A Call for Action," U.S. Mission to the European Union, November 2010.

[5] Declaration of the New Transatlantic Agenda at the U.S.-EU Summit, December 13, 1995.

[6] Joint statement of the delegations of the U.S. Congress and the European Parliament, January 16, 1999.

[7] CRS interviews with congressional staff.

[8] *Resetting The Trans-Atlantic Economic Council, A BluePrint,* A Report by the Atlantic Council and Bertelsmann Foundation, October 2009.

[9] *Shoulder to Shoulder: Forging a Strategic U.S.-EU Partnership*, Atlantic Council of the United States, Center for Transatlantic Relations et al., December 2009.

[10] The EP's 41 delegations consist of 37 interparliamentary delegations (some are termed either Joint Parliamentary Committees or Parliamentary Cooperation Committees) that maintain relations with countries and regions around the world ranging from Russia to China to the Middle East, and four delegations to parliamentary assemblies (such as the Euro-Latin American Parliamentary Assembly). For a list of current EP delegations, see the website of the European Parliament, http://www.europarl.europa.eu.

[11] CRS interviews with congressional staff.

[12] CRS interviews with representatives of the business community.

[13] European Parliament resolution (A6-0114/2009) adopted March 26, 2009.

[14] As of December 1, 2009, and as a result of the ratification of the EU's Lisbon Treaty, the Commission's Washington office is now referred to as the "Delegation of the European Union."

[15] For more information, see the EPLO website, http://www.europarl.europa.eu/us.

[16] Judy Schneider, Senior Specialist on the Congress in CRS' Government and Finance Division contributed information on the U.S. committee system for this section. For more information, see CRS Report RS20794, *The Committee System in the U.S. Congress*, by Judy Schneider.

[17] In some policy areas, such as tax matters, social security, and most aspects of foreign and defense policy, EU member states retain decision-making authority and the Parliament does not have the right of "co-decision," although it may give a non-binding opinion.

In: Congress and the European Parliament
Editors D. J. Armstrong et al.
ISBN: 978-1-62100-748-7
©2012 Nova Science Publishers, Inc.

Chapter 2

THE EUROPEAN PARLIAMENT[1]

Kristin Archick and Derek E. Mix

SUMMARY

The 736-member European Parliament (EP) is a key institution of the European Union (EU), a unique political and economic partnership composed of 27 member states. The EP is the only EU institution that is directly elected. The EP plays a role in the EU's legislative and budgeting processes, and works closely with the two other main EU bodies, the European Commission and the Council of the European Union (also known as the Council of Ministers). Although the EP does not formally initiate EU legislation, it shares legislative power with the Council of Ministers in many policy areas, giving it the right to accept, amend, or reject proposed EU laws.

Members of the European Parliament (MEPs) serve five-year terms. The most recent EP elections were held in June 2009. The EP currently has seven political groups, which caucus according to political ideology rather than nationality, plus a number of "non-attached" or independent members. The EP

---

[1] This is an edited, reformatted and augmented version of Congressional Research Service RS21998.

has 20 standing committees that are key actors in the adoption of EU legislation and a total of 41 delegations that maintain international parliament-to-parliament relations. The EP is led by a President, who oversees its work and represents the EP externally.

Once limited to being a consultative assembly, the EP has accumulated more power over time. Experts assert that the EU's latest effort at institutional reform—the Lisbon Treaty, which entered into force on December 1, 2009—significantly increases the relative power of the EP within the EU. The Lisbon Treaty gives the EP a say equal to that of the member states in the Council of Ministers over the vast majority of EU legislation (with some exceptions in areas such as tax matters and foreign policy), as well as the right to decide on the allocation of the EU budget jointly with the Council. The treaty also gives the EP the power to approve or reject international agreements and expands the EP's decision-making authority over trade-related issues.

Many analysts note that the EP has not been shy about exerting its new powers under the Lisbon Treaty, and in some areas, with implications for U.S. interests. In February 2010, the EP rejected the U.S.-EU SWIFT agreement allowing U.S. authorities access to European financial data to help counter terrorism. Although the EP eventually approved a revised U.S.-EU SWIFT accord in July 2010, it did so only after several EP demands related to strengthening data privacy protections were agreed to by the United States and the other EU institutions.

Although supporters point to the EP's growing institutional clout, others assert that the EP still faces several challenges of public perception. Skeptics contend that the EP lacks the legitimacy of national parliaments and that its powers remain somewhat limited. Some analysts observe that the complexity of the EU legislative process contributes to limited public interest and understanding of the EP's role, leading to declining turnout in European Parliament elections and wider charges of a democratic deficit in the EU. Criticism has also been directed at the costs incurred by what many consider duplicate EP facilities in several European cities.

Ties between the EP and the U.S. Congress are long-standing, and institutional cooperation currently exists through the Transatlantic Legislators' Dialogue. In light of the EP's new powers following the entrance into force of the Lisbon Treaty, the EP and its activities may be of increasing interest to the 112th Congress.

THE EUROPEAN PARLIAMENT: A KEY EU INSTITUTION

The 736-member European Parliament (EP) is a key institution of the European Union (EU). The EU is a political and economic partnership that represents a unique form of cooperation among its 27 member states.[1] The EU is the latest stage of a process of European integration begun in the 1950s to promote peace and economic prosperity in Europe; the EU has been built through a series of binding treaties, and its members have committed to harmonizing laws and adopting common policies on an extensive range of issues. EU member states work together through common institutions to set policy and promote their collective interests.

As the only EU institution that is directly elected, the European Parliament represents the citizens of the EU. Once limited to being a consultative assembly, the EP has accumulated more power over time. Successive EU treaties have enhanced the EP's role and responsibilities in order to improve democratic accountability in the EU policy-making process. Experts assert that the EU's new Lisbon Treaty—which took effect on December 1, 2009—has increased the relative power of the EP within the EU significantly. The Lisbon Treaty contains a wide range of internal reforms aimed at improving the effectiveness of the EU's governing institutions, increasing democratic transparency within the EU, and giving the EU a more coherent voice and identity on the world stage. Among other measures, the Lisbon Treaty strengthens the EP's role in the EU's legislative and budgeting processes. Many Members of the European Parliament (MEPs) view the EP as one of the big "winners" of this latest round of EU institutional reform.

> ## OTHER EU INSTITUTIONS
>
> The ***European Commission*** upholds the common interest of the Union as a whole. It is independent of the member states' national governments. As the EU's executive, the Commission has the sole right of legislative initiative in most cases and implements EU decisions and common policies. It also serves as the guardian of the EU's treaties, ensuring that member states adopt and abide by their provisions. The 27 Commissioners, one from each EU country, are appointed by agreement among the member states to five-year terms. One Commissioner serves as Commission President. Each of the other Commissioners holds a distinct portfolio (e.g., agriculture, energy, trade), similar to U.S. department secretaries and agency directors.
>
> The ***Council of the European Union (Council of Ministers)*** represents the national governments of the 27 member states. The Council enacts legislation based on proposals put forward by the Commission and agreed to (in most cases) by the Parliament; in some sensitive areas such as taxation and foreign policy, however, the Council retains decision-making authority. A minister from each country takes part in Council meetings, with participation configured according to the subject under consideration (e.g., agriculture ministers would meet to discuss farm subsidies). The Presidency of the Council rotates among the member states, changing every six months.
>
> The ***European Council*** brings together the Heads of State or Government of the member states and the President of the European Commission at least four times a year (in what are often termed "EU Summits"). It acts principally as a guide and driving force for EU policy. The European Council is headed by a President, who serves as the coordinator and spokesman for the work of the 27 Heads of State or Government.
>
> The ***Court of Justice*** interprets EU law, and its rulings are binding. The *Court of Auditors* monitors the Union's financial management. A number of other *advisory committees* represent economic, social, and regional interests.

The EP also works closely with the two other main EU institutions—the European Commission and the Council of the European Union (also known as the Council of Ministers). Despite the EP's growing power and influence, the

EP is not widely considered a legislative body in the traditional sense because it cannot initiate legislation; that right rests largely with the Commission, which functions as the EU's executive.[2] The Council, which is composed of ministers from the national governments, adopts legislation jointly with the Parliament (in most cases) based on proposals put forward by the Commission. Thus, the EP has an important right to accept, amend, or reject proposed EU legislation.

ROLE OF THE EUROPEAN PARLIAMENT

Legislative Process

The role of the European Parliament in the legislative process has expanded steadily over time as the scope of EU policy has grown. Initially limited to offering non-binding opinions in a "consultation procedure," the EP gained more power to affect EU legislation in the "cooperation procedure" of the 1986 Single European Act. The EP's role in the EU's legislative process, especially in areas related to the EU's common internal market, was increased further by the introduction of the "co-decision procedure" in the Maastricht Treaty of 1992. In the "co-decision procedure," the EP and the Council of Ministers share legislative power and must both approve a Commission proposal for it to become EU law. The Amsterdam Treaty of 1997 extended the use of "co-decision" to many additional policy areas (ranging from the environment to social policy). As more decisions within the Council of Ministers have become subject to a complex majority voting system rather than unanimity to allow for greater speed and efficiency of decision-making, the Parliament's right of "co-decision" has come to be viewed as an increasingly important democratic counterweight at the European level to the Commission and Council.[3]

As noted above, the Lisbon Treaty strengthens the EP's responsibilities, especially in the EU's legislative process. It roughly doubles the Parliament's right of "co-decision" to almost 80 policy areas, including agriculture and justice and home affairs issues such as immigration and police cooperation. In doing so, the Lisbon Treaty gives the EP a say—equal to that of the member states in the Council of Ministers—over the vast majority of legislation passed in the EU. Tax matters, social security, and most aspects of foreign policy, however, are among the areas in which EU member states retain decision-making authority and to which the "co-decision procedure" does not apply (the

Parliament may give a non-binding opinion). The Lisbon Treaty technically renames the "co-decision procedure" as the "ordinary legislative procedure," although the term "co-decision" continues to be used frequently in practice.

> ### THE "CO-DECISION PROCEDURE"
>
> The EU's "ordinary legislative procedure," or "co-decision," can be summarized as follows: (1) if Parliament and the Council of Ministers agree on a Commission proposal, it is approved; (2) if they disagree, the Council forms a common position; the EP can then either accept the Council's common position, or reject or amend it, by an absolute majority of its members; (3) if the Council cannot accept the EP's amendments, a conciliation meeting is convened, after which the EP and the Council approve an agreement if one can be reached. If they are unable to agree, the proposal is not adopted.

Additionally, in the "consent procedure," the EP must, by a simple "yes" or "no" majority, approve the accession of new EU member states and the conclusion of agreements with third parties, such as association and trade agreements with non-member states.[4] If the Parliament does not give its consent, such agreements cannot enter into force.

Budgetary Process

The EP and the Council of Ministers together constitute the EU's budget authority and are responsible for allocating the EU's annual budget; they decide, for example, on the amount of funding dedicated to infrastructure as opposed to education. However, neither the EP nor the Council can affect the size of the EU's annual budget; that amount is fixed periodically by agreement among the EU's member states as a percentage of the Union's combined gross national income (GNI).[5] The EU's 2011 budget is EUR 141.9 billion (approximately $190 billion).

With the entrance into force of the Lisbon Treaty, the Parliament has the right to decide on the allocation of the entire EU budget jointly with the Council. Previously, the EP had the last word on "non-compulsory" expenditures, such as development aid, but the Council had the final say on "compulsory" expenditures, such as spending related to agriculture or international agreements. The Lisbon Treaty eliminates the dis-tinction between "compulsory" and "non-compulsory" expenditures. Of particular importance, the EP gains more control over agricultural spending, which usually accounts for over one-third of the EU's annual budget.

Under the Lisbon Treaty, the EU's annual budgetary procedure begins with the Commission proposing a draft budget. The Council adopts its position on the draft budget, including any amendments, and sends it to the EP for its consideration. The Parliament then has 42 days to either approve the draft budget or amend it and send it back to the Council. If the Council agrees with the EP's amendments, the budget is adopted; if the Council disagrees with the EP's changes, a Conciliation Committee is convened to resolve differences and reach agreement on a joint text within 21 days. The joint text must then be approved by both the Council and the EP; however, if the joint text is rejected by the Council, the EP—subject to certain conditions—ultimately has the right to approve the budget. In the event that both the EP and the Council reject the joint text or fail to decide, the Commission must submit a new draft budget. Some EP advocates assert that the EP's position in the annual budgetary process is now stronger than that of the Council, as the Council may never impose a budget against the will of the EP, but under some circumstances, the EP may impose a budget against the will of the Council; at the same time, most experts agree that in practice, the EP would likely only exert this right in exceptional situations.[6]

In determining the EU's annual budget, the EP and the Council must also adhere to annual spending limits laid out in the EU's multi-annual financial framework, which defines the long-term political priorities for the EU and sets annual maximum amounts for each priority and expenditure category.[7] According to the Lisbon Treaty, the Council must agree unanimously on each multiannual financial framework, after having obtained the Parliament's consent. As such, the Parliament has a degree of input into the EU's overall budgetary direction and the ability to help shape the EU budget to reflect its own political priorities.

In addition, the EP examines the European Commission's implementation of previous annual budgets through the "discharge procedure." In order to close the budget books of a given year, the EP must vote to grant "discharge" based on reports of the EU Court of Auditors and a recommendation of the Council. With its decision, the EP also presents the Commission with binding recommendations and observations regarding implementation of the budget.

The EP's budgetary powers are considerably greater than those exercised by most parliaments in EU member states.

Supervision and Oversight Responsibilities

The Parliament has a supervisory role over the European Commission and exercises some limited oversight over the activities of the Council of Ministers. The EP monitors the management of EU policies, can conduct investigations and public hearings, and may submit oral and written questions to the Commission and the Council. The Presidency of the Council, which rotates among the member states every six months, presents its program to the Parliament at the beginning of its term and reports on results achieved at the end of its mandate.

Of particular note, the EP plays a role in the approval process of each new Commission and Commission President every five years. According to the Lisbon Treaty, the member states agree together (usually during a meeting of the European Council) on who to designate as the Commission President, and their selection must take into account the results of the most recent EP elections. Thus, the relative strengths of the political groups in the EP (see below for more information) can affect who is nominated by the member states to this post. The nominee for Commission President then must be "elected" by a majority vote in the EP.

Analysts note that this "election" procedure is largely intended to raise public awareness of the importance of EP elections and the EP's role in choosing the Commission President; in practice, they assert, it differs very little from the previous parliamentary "approval" process. For example, in both 2004 and 2009—that is, before the Lisbon Treaty's entrance into force— the EP's strongest political group successfully demanded that the Commission President be of the same political stripe. At the same time, given that no single political group in the EP has ever held a majority on its own, the support of other political groups has always been needed in order to approve the nomination. In September 2009, the EP supported the re-appointment of 2004-2009 Commission President José Manuel Barroso for the 2009-2014 term (by a vote of 382 to 219, with 117 abstentions).[8]

The EP also has the power to accept or reject a newly proposed Commission as a whole, but not individual nominees. Since 1995, the EP has held U.S. Senate-style confirmation hearings for newly designated Commissioners, who are nominated by the member states. In February 2010, the EP voted to approve the so-called Barroso II Commission for the term ending in 2014. Although a new Commission was supposed to have been in place by November 2009, it was held up because of delays in the ratification of the Lisbon Treaty by some member states. The confirmation process for the new Commission was further slowed when the initial Bulgarian nominee withdrew her candidacy in mid-January 2010 after a contentious hearing before the Parliament amid concerns about her past financial dealings and her competence for her portfolio. A similar situation occurred in 2004, when the EP essentially forced the original Italian nominee to the Commission to withdraw due to concerns about his views on homosexuality and women's rights. Some observers view these episodes as signs of the EP's growing confidence and institutional clout.

In addition, the EP may dismiss the entire Commission (although, again, not individual Commissioners) through a vote of censure. To date, the EP has never adopted a motion of censure. However, in 1999, the entire Commission opted to resign rather than face a formal censure by the EP over alleged corruption charges.

ORGANIZATION OF THE EUROPEAN PARLIAMENT

Members of the European Parliament serve five-year terms, and have been directly elected since 1979.[9] Voting for the EP takes place on a national basis, with the number of MEPs elected in each country based roughly on population size. Germany, for example, has the largest number of MEPs (99), while Malta has the smallest (5).

The most recent EP elections were held on June 4-7, 2009, with 736 seats at stake.[10] Roughly 375 million European citizens were eligible to cast a ballot in 2009. In EP elections, EU citizens may vote—or run for a seat—in their country of residence, without necessarily holding citizenship in that country. Turnout has declined in every EP election, from 63% in 1979 to a new low of 43% in 2009. Although the overall number is comparable to turnout in U.S. mid-term elections, some analysts contend that relatively low voter participation compared to national elections indicates a lack of awareness and understanding about the EP.

Political Groups

Once elected, Members of the European Parliament caucus according to transnational groups based on political ideology, rather than by nationality. A political group must consist of at least 25 MEPs from a minimum of seven EU member states. The EP currently has seven political groups—containing over 100 individual political parties—plus a number of "non-attached" or independent members.

Each group appoints a chair or co-chairs, and maintains a bureau and secretariat to manage its internal organization. Prior to a vote, MEPs within each group study the legislative proposals in question with the support of committee reports, discuss prospective amendments, and seek to arrive at a consensus group position. However, individual MEPs are not bound to vote according to their group's position.

Table 1. Political Groups and Seats in the European Parliament: Results of the 2009 Election (736 seats total).

	Total Seats	%
European People's Party [Christian Democrats] (EPP; center-right)	265	36
Progressive Alliance of Socialists and Democrats in the European Parliament (S&D; center-left/socialists)	184	25
Alliance of Liberals and Democrats for Europe (ALDE; centrist/liberals)	84	11.4
Greens/European Free Alliance (Greens-EFA; greens and regionalists)	55	7.5
European Conservatives and Reformists (ECR; right-wing, anti-Federalist)	54	7.3
European United Left/Nordic Green Left (GUE-NGL; far-left and former communists)	35	4.8
Europe of Freedom and Democracy (EFD; euroskeptics)	32	4.3
Non-attached members	27	3.7

Source: http://www.europarl.europa.eu/parliament/archive/elections2009/en/index_en.html.
Note: Percentages are rounded.

As noted previously, no single group has ever held an absolute majority in the European Parliament, making compromise and coalition-building important elements of the legislative process. Some analysts assert that distinct ideological definitions between groups are becoming more complicated, as voting blocs form increasingly according to specific issues and interests. Nevertheless, the two largest groups have tended to dominate the Parliament historically.

In the 2009 elections, the *Group of the European People's Party [Christian Democrats] (EPP)* retained its position as the largest political group in the EP with 265 seats. The EPP is center-right in political orientation. In relative terms, the strength of the EPP in the 2009 elections increased significantly due to a sizeable drop in support for center-left parties. Although circumstances and issues differed in each EU member state, some analysts interpreted these results as indicating greater public preference for the approaches of conservative and center-right parties in the handling of the global financial crisis and recession. However, the center-left *Group of the Progressive Alliance of Socialists and Democrats in the European Parliament (S&D)*, with 184 seats, remains the EP's second-largest political group following the 2009 elections.

The EPP and the S&D have a history of cross-ideological legislative partnership. As in the 2004-2009 EP (in which the S&D was called the PES—the Socialist Group in the European Parliament), the two parties continue to cooperate closely in an unofficial "Grand Coalition" and together frequently shape politics in the EP. Critics argue that the consensus-seeking of the "Grand Coalition" makes politics in the EP stale and paradoxical. Other observers note that maximizing consensus and unity lends the EP greater institutional weight. As a general rule, most MEPs prefer consensus outcomes that are endorsed by a large and broad majority.

The third-largest group in the EP is the *Group of the Alliance of Liberals and Democrats for Europe (ALDE)*. ALDE, with 84 seats, is centrist and liberal in political orientation. In European political terminology, "liberal" connotes an emphasis on free market economics, individual rights, social equality, and de-centralized government. In the past, ALDE was often viewed as the "kingmaker," able to exercise a decisive swing vote for a majority in the EP. However, as a result of some losses suffered by ALDE in the 2009 elections and the shift of the political balance in the EP largely to the right, some analysts assert that ALDE's political capital has decreased. Other observers contend that as the third-largest group, ALDE's position on a given issue will still be a crucial factor in the outcome of many EP votes.

The remaining four political groups in the EP are smaller in size, ranging from 32 to 55 members each. On the left side of the political spectrum are the *Group of the Greens/European Free Alliance (Greens-EFA)*; and the *Confederal Group of the European United Left/Nordic Green Left (GUE-*

NGL). The Greens-EFA is largely comprised of numerous European Green parties—leftist in political orientation with a strong emphasis on pro-environment politics and human rights—and several regional parties (e.g., Scottish, Welsh, Basque, and Catalonian) with a leftist or center-left outlook. Despite the overall trend in the EP to the right in the 2009 elections, the Greens-EFA attracted many voters who sought change, resulting in a significant increase in the number of their seats. The GUE-NGL consists of parties that are even farther left in orientation; some have a Green emphasis while others have roots in communism. The GUE-NGL is pro-EU and pro-integration, but strongly critical of existing EU structures, policies, and overall direction.

On the right side of the political spectrum are two new groups: the *European Conservatives and Reformists Group (ECR)*; and the *Europe of Freedom and Democracy Group (EFD)*. The ECR was formed in 2009, after the UK Conservative Party broke with the EPP amid growing unease with the EPP's support for continued EU integration. The ECR is right-wing in political orientation and strongly opposed to a "federalist" Europe. Even farther to the right is the EFD, composed of "euroskeptics" and critics of the EU who oppose further European integration.

Many of the "non-attached" or independent members of the EP hail from far-right extremist parties, which made gains in the 2009 EP elections in a number of countries, such as the Netherlands, Austria, and Hungary. However, these far-right MEPs still hold a relatively small number of seats and appear to have little cohesion among themselves. Analysts note that they have been unable to form a political group and as a result are likely to have minimal impact in the current EP; membership in a political group gives MEPs more influence as groups receive more funding and more speaking time in the EP than do non-attached members.[11]

COMPOSITION OF POLITICAL GROUPS IN THE EUROPEAN PARLIAMENT

European People's Party (EPP). The center-right EPP contains MEPs from Germany's Christian Democratic/Christian Social Union (CDU-CSU), France's Union pour un Mouvement Populaire (UMP), Spain's Partido Popular (PP), Italy's People of Freedom, Poland's Civic Platform, and numerous other Christian Democratic, conservative, center-right, and centrist national parties. The chair of the EPP is French MEP Joseph Daul.

Progressive Alliance of Socialists and Democrats in the European Parliament (S&D). The center-left S&D includes MEPs from Germany's Social Democratic Party (SPD), France's Socialist Party, the UK Labour Party, Spain's Socialist Party, and numerous other Socialist, Social Democratic, and center-left parties. The chair of S&D is German MEP Martin Schulz.

Alliance of Liberals and Democrats for Europe (ALDE). MEPs in the centrist ALDE hail from the UK Liberal Democrat Party, Germany's Free Democrat Party (FDP), and Ireland's Fianna Fail. The chair of ALDE is Belgian MEP (and former Belgian Prime Minister) Guy Verhofstadt.

Greens/European Free Alliance (Greens-EFA). The leftist and pro-environment Greens-EFA includes MEPs from Germany's Alliance '90/The Greens, France's Europe Ecologie, and the Scottish National Party. The co-chairs of the Greens-EFA are French MEP Daniel Cohn-Bendit and German MEP Rebecca Harms.

European Conservatives and Reformists (ECR). The largest number of MEPs in the right-wing ECR are from the UK Conservative Party, Poland's Law and Justice Party, and the Czech Republic's Civic Democratic Party. The chair of ECR is Polish MEP Michal Kaminski.

European United Left/Nordic Green Left (GUE-NGL). The far-left GUE-NGL contains MEPs from Germany's Die Linke, the French Communist Party, and the Irish party Sinn Fein. The chair of GUE-NGL is German MEP Lothar Bisky.

Europe of Freedom and Democracy (EFD). The largest contingents in the euroskeptic EFD are from the UK Independence Party (UKIP), which advocates UK withdrawal from the EU, and Italy's Lega Nord. The co-chairs of EFD are British MEP Nigel Farage and Italian MEP Francesco Enrico Speroni.

Note: This box is meant for illustrative purposes; it is not a definitive or exhaustive list of all the political parties comprising each political group in the European Parliament.

The EP President

Every two-and-a-half years (twice per parliamentary term), MEPs vote to elect a President of the European Parliament. The majority coalition in the EP (previously and currently an EPP "Grand Coalition" with the Socialists) has traditionally agreed to split the position of EP president over each five-year term. At the opening session of the new EP in mid-July 2009, Members elected Polish MEP Jerzy Buzek of the EPP as President. Buzek, a former prime minister of Poland, is the first ever EP President from one of the central and eastern European member countries that joined the EU in 2004. Martin Schulz of S&D is expected to take over as EP President for the second half of the EP's current term.

The President of the EP represents the EP externally and in relations with the other EU institutions. The President oversees the work of the Parliament and is responsible for ensuring that its rules of procedure are followed. The President is assisted in managing the Parliament's internal organization and affairs by a Bureau composed of 14 Vice-Presidents and five Quaestors (responsible for administrative and financial matters) drawn from across the EP's political groups. The signature of the President is the final step in approval of the EU budget, and the President cosigns, together with the President of the Council, legislation adopted under the co-decision procedure. In addition, the President seeks to affect broader EU policies by promoting a few key issues as EP priorities. Since his election, Buzek has stressed employment, energy security and the environment, foreign policy and human rights, and EP reform as his presidency priorities.

Committees

The EP has 20 standing committees, each addressing specific issues such as education, the environment, and economic and monetary affairs. The EP may also set up subcommittees and special committees, which investigate or oversee specific issues for a limited period of time. For example, in 2006, the EP established a special committee to examine the role of EU member states in hosting secret CIA detention facilities and aiding CIA flights related to the rendition of terrorism suspects. Currently, the EP has two special committees, focusing respectively on the EU's response to the global financial crisis and the EU's next multiannual financial framework. Only one EP committee—the foreign affairs committee—has subcommittees (one focuses on human rights, the other on security and defense issues).

EP committees vary in size, usually containing from 20 to 80 MEPs. Each committee has a chairman, four vice-chairmen, and a secretariat to guide its work. The political make-up of the committees reflects that of the EP as a whole, and committee posts are allocated proportionally to the respective size of the political groups; for example, the EPP currently chairs nine committees, the S&D seven, and the ALDE three.

EP committees are key actors in the adoption of EU legislation. In terms of their importance and strength, EP committees rival those in the U.S. Congress and surpass the role of committees in most national European legislatures. EP committees consider legislative proposals put forward by the Commission and the Council of Ministers. The appropriate committee (e.g., the Committee on the Environment, Public Health, and Food Safety would deal with legislation on pollution) appoints a MEP as "rapporteur" to draft a report on the legislative proposal under consideration. The rapporteur submits a draft report to the committee for discussion, which the committee then votes on and possibly amends. The committee's report is then considered in a plenary session of the entire Parliament, amended if necessary, and put to a vote. The EP thus adopts its position on the proposed EU legislation. Committees may also draw up their "own initiative" reports, in which they recommend action in a particular area by the Commission or the member states.

Delegations

The European Parliament plays a role in the EU's international presence through a total of 41 delegations that range in size; most have between 20 and 50 MEPs. These delegations maintain parliament-to-parliament contacts and relations with representatives of many countries and regions around the world. For example, the EP has interparliamentary delegations for relations with the United States and the NATO Parliamentary Assembly, as well as with Russia, Iran, Israel, the Palestinian Legislative Council, China, India, and the Korean Peninsula.

Administration

A Secretariat of almost 5,000 non-partisan civil servants provides administrative and technical support to the Parliament. In addition, MEPs and political groups have their own staffs.

Location and Schedule

Strasbourg, France (near the German border) is the official seat of the EP; plenary sessions are held there for one week a month. For two weeks a month, the EP's standing committees meet 300 miles to the northwest in Brussels, Belgium, where the European Commission and the Council of Ministers are located. There are also occasional "part plenary" sessions (two days) in Brussels. One week each month is set aside for meetings of the political groups, which are usually held in Brussels. MEPs must have offices and lodgings in both cities. The EP's Secretariat is based in both Brussels and Luxembourg, which is about mid-way between Strasbourg and Brussels.

Languages

Simultaneous interpretation of all parliamentary and committee debates is provided in the EU's 23 official languages. All parliamentary documents are translated into 21 of these languages (Irish and Maltese are sometimes excepted), and some documents must be translated into all 23. Such extensive translation and publication services represent significant administrative costs. However, many EU and EP officials consider such costs to be a price worth paying, both on democratic grounds—to enable MEPs to scrutinize and vote on draft EU laws in the languages they understand best—and on grounds of cultural and linguistic diversity within the Union.

GROWING INFLUENCE AND ONGOING CHALLENGES

As noted previously, EP advocates assert that "co-decision" and its institutional supervisory roles have substantially enhanced the Parliament's influence. The Lisbon Treaty, in effect, gives the EP veto authority over the vast majority of EU legislation and a greater say over the EU's budget. In addition, the Lisbon Treaty gives the EP the right to approve or reject all international agreements by a simple majority and expands the EP's decision-making authority over trade-related issues.

Analysts observe that the EP has not been shy about exerting its new powers under the Lisbon Treaty, and in some cases, with significant implications for U.S. interests. In February 2010, by a vote of 378 to 196 (with 31 abstentions), the EP rejected a U.S.-EU accord aimed at countering terrorism; the so-called SWIFT agreement, negotiated by the Commission and approved by the Council of Ministers, would have continued allowing U.S. authorities access to European financial data in an effort to help prevent or investigate terrorist attacks. Prior to the Lisbon Treaty, the EP did not have the authority to veto such an accord. Many MEPs had long claimed that the U.S.-EU SWIFT agreement did not contain sufficient protections to safeguard the personal data and privacy rights of EU citizens. In addition, some MEPs reportedly sought to send a message to the Commission and Council, conveying that the EP's position must now be taken into account during (and not after) the negotiation of international agreements or the drafting of new legislative proposals. Although the EP eventually approved a revised U.S.-EU SWIFT agreement in July 2010, it did so only after several EP demands related to strengthening data privacy protections were agreed to by the United States, the European Commission, and the Council of Ministers.[12]

Supporters also claim that the EP's influence has been growing even in consultative areas, such as the EU's common foreign policy, where the "co-decision procedure" does not apply and where decisions rest largely with the member states. They maintain that the EP has become a forum for debate on international issues, and uses its power of consent on cooperation accords with third parties and Parliamentary resolutions to promote its views and highlight issues such as human rights. For example, many observers credit the EP's opposition in 2005 to ending the EU's arms embargo on China (on both human rights and strategic grounds) as one factor that eventually dissuaded member states from lifting the embargo. More recently, some experts assert that the agreement reached between the EP and the other EU institutions on the establishment of the European External Action Service (EEAS)—the new EU diplomatic corps called for by the Lisbon Treaty—has the potential to greatly increase the EP's voice in the foreign policy realm. The EP fought for and largely won considerable oversight of the EEAS by demanding scrutiny over its political appointments, staffing, and budget.

Nevertheless, the European Parliament faces several challenges of public perception. Some skeptics contend that the EP, despite being a directly elected body, lacks the legitimacy of national parliaments. They argue that the EU's legislative process is overly complex and often focused on highly technical issues, leading to a lack of public understanding about the role of the EP. Limited public awareness of the EP's activities, they maintain, is reflected in the consistently declining turnout in European Parliament elections, which in turn, feeds back into skepticism of the EP's legitimacy as a representative institution and fuels wider charges of a democratic deficit and a lack of transparency in EU policy-making.

Closely related to the question of the EP's legitimacy is the issue of whether MEPs reflect national or European interests. Studies on voting behavior in the EP have shown that ideology holds greater influence than nationality, with MEPs voting with their party groups the vast majority of the time. On the other hand, some observers contend that MEPs at times promote parochial national interests. Past examples include Italian and Spanish MEPs defending olive growers, and British and Irish MEPs joining forces to oppose tax harmonization measures. And some point out that many MEPs campaign on national rather than European issues. Many voters view EP elections as a national mid-term election—an indication of voter opinion on the performance of the national government—rather than as a vote on Europe-wide issues.[13]

Another major concern is costs, which the EP has long been under public pressure to reduce. The fact that MEPs and their staffs regularly shuttle between three cities leads to travel and hotel bills that, in the past, have consumed a sizeable portion of the EP's budget. Yet, the suggestion that the EP should consolidate its operations in one city has met with strong opposition in the host countries of France, Belgium, and Luxembourg, which fear the loss of symbolism and prestige, in addition to jobs and other economic benefits. The French city of Strasbourg, which is close to the German border, was originally chosen as the seat of the EP to serve as a symbol of peace and reconciliation between the two countries, and both argue it should continue to do so. Construction of multi-million-dollar buildings in Brussels and Strasbourg in the late 1990s to accommodate the growth in MEPs following EU enlargement also stirred public controversy, as did the former flat-rate expense regime for MEPs that some viewed as contributing to the EP's "gravy train" image (the EP instituted a reimbursable system for business and travel expenses in 2009).

Finally, a number of analysts suggest that the enhanced powers granted to the EP by the Lisbon Treaty, and the EP's resulting new-found assertiveness, could lead to greater inter-institutional rivalry within the EU and make the EU's legislative process even more complex. As noted above, the EP complicated the approval of the U.S.-EU SWIFT agreement, and some observers contend that EP maneuvering regarding the EEAS has delayed its establishment. Other commentators anticipate that the European Commission or the Council of Ministers, anxious to protect their own institutional turf, may challenge some EP actions in the EU Court of Justice. For example, press reports indicate that the Council of Ministers believes that some provisions of a new EP-European Commission framework agreement (governing relations between the two bodies) are not in line with the EU treaties, and has threatened to submit a complaint to the Court.[14]

THE EUROPEAN PARLIAMENT AND THE U.S. CONGRESS[15]

Ties between the EP and the U.S. Congress date back to 1972, when a U.S. congressional delegation first visited the EP in Brussels and Luxembourg. Since then, with a few exceptions, congressional-EP exchanges have taken place twice a year, and have provided the opportunity for sustained dialogue. The U.S. Congress-EP exchange is the oldest and widely considered the most prestigious of the EP's interparliamentary dialogues.

In 1999, the EP and the U.S. Congress launched the Transatlantic Legislators' Dialogue (TLD) as their official response to the U.S.-EU commitment in the 1995 New Transatlantic Agenda to enhance parliamentary ties between the EU and the United States. With the TLD, the two sides have committed to regular meetings twice a year to discuss a wide range of topical political and economic issues. In the EP, the TLD is led by a chairman and EP participants in the semi-annual TLD meetings are drawn from the EP's Delegation for Relations with the United States. In the Congress, the TLD is headed by a chair and two vice-chairs and U.S. participants are from the House only. The most recent TLD meeting took place in December 2010 in San Francisco, California (the venue for the TLD usually alternates between the United States and Europe). Congress and the EP have also conducted video conferences on specific areas of mutual concern. However, some U.S. analysts observe that the TLD remains relatively obscure in the Congress, with ambiguity regarding which Members actually belong, and no role given to the U.S. Senate.

Many MEPs would like to enhance cooperation with the U.S. Congress further. In March 2009, the EP adopted a resolution, which among other measures, asserted that the U.S. Congress and the EP should promote closer ties between legislative committees and should create a reciprocal legislative "early-warning" system to identify potential legislative activities that could affect relations between the United States and the EU. In January 2010, the EP established a liaison office with the U.S. Congress in Washington, DC; EP staffers deployed as part of this office will seek to keep the EP better informed of legislative activity in the U.S. House and Senate by attending hearings, following legislation, and establishing working relationships with Members of Congress, committees, and their staffs. The EP also hopes that the U.S. Congress will consider the possibility of setting up a similar congressional liaison office in Brussels.[16]

End Notes

[1] The 27 member states of the EU are: Austria, Belgium, Bulgaria, Cyprus, the Czech Republic, Denmark, Estonia, Finland, France, Germany, Greece, Hungary, Ireland, Italy, Latvia, Lithuania, Luxembourg, Malta, the Netherlands, Poland, Portugal, Romania, Slovakia, Slovenia, Spain, Sweden, and the United Kingdom.

[2] EP supporters contend that the EP has a limited power of political initiative; the EP can ask the Commission to introduce a legislative proposal, but the Commission is not required to comply with the EP's request.

[3] The voting system in the Council of Ministers is known as Qualified Majority Voting (QMV); each EU member state is allotted a number of votes in rough proportion to its population size. Passage of a measure currently requires at least half of the member states and 255 out of the 345 total votes, representing at least 62% of the EU population. Under the Lisbon Treaty, a simpler formula for QMV will be introduced in 2014 but not fully implemented until 2017.

[4] Prior to the entry into force of the Lisbon Treaty, the "consent procedure" was known as the "assent procedure."

[5] Currently, EU member states have set an annual budget ceiling of 1.29% of the Union's gross national income. The EU budget comes from three main sources: external customs duties; a share of each member state's value added tax (VAT) revenue; and a further contribution from each member state based on the size of its individual GNI.

[6] See Fact Sheets on the European Union, "The Budgetary Procedure," available on the website of the European Parliament, http://www.europarl.europa.eu.

[7] The EU's current multiannual financial framework covers the period 2007-2013.

[8] Barroso, from Portugal, is a former prime minister from a conservative Portuguese political party. As such, he was backed in both 2004 and 2009 for Commission President by the EP's largest political group, which is center-right in political orientation. See also, Sebastian Kurpas, "The Treaty of Lisbon: How Much 'Constitution' Is Left?," *CEPS Policy Brief*, December 2007.

[9] Prior to direct elections, MEPs were appointed by their national parliaments.

[10] The Lisbon Treaty sets the number of MEPs at 751 starting in 2014. With the Lisbon Treaty now ratified, it is expected that 18 additional MEPs will be added to the EP, temporarily raising the number of MEPs for the current term to 754.

[11] "Voters Steer Europe to the Right," BBC News, June 8, 2009; Stephen Castle, "Far Right Is Left Out at EU's Assembly," *International Herald Tribune*, July 15, 2009; Julia De Clerck-Sachsse, "The New European Parliament: All Change or Business as Usual?," *CEPS Special Report*, August 2009.

[12] "MEPs Hail Historic Rejection of SWIFT Deal," *Agence Europe*, February 13, 2010; "SWIFT: Rapporteur Announces Last-Minute Agreement," *Europolitics*, June 25, 2010. For more information on the SWIFT accord, see CRS Report RS22030, *U.S.-EU Cooperation Against Terrorism*, by Kristin Archick.

[13] Simon Hix and Abdul Noury, "After Enlargement: Voting Patterns in the Sixth European Parliament," *Legislative Studies Quarterly*, May 2009; Julia De Clerck-Sachsse and Piotr Maciej Kaczynski, "The European Parliament: More Powerful, Less Legitimate," *CEPS Working Document*, May 2009.

[14] "EP/Commission: Council Challenges Framework Agreement," *Agence Europe*, October 23, 2010.

[15] For more information, see CRS Report R41552, *The U.S. Congress and the European Parliament: Evolving Transatlantic Legislative Cooperation*, by Kristin Archick and Vincent Morelli. Also see the European Parliament's website on the Transatlantic Legislators' Dialogue, http://www.europarl.europa.eu/intcoop/tld/default_en.htm.

[16] European Parliament resolution (A6-0114/2009), adopted March 26, 2009.

INDEX

A

accounting, 6, 21, 28
Afghanistan, 3
agencies, 12, 13
agriculture, 5, 9, 26, 28, 44, 45, 47
Amsterdam Treaty, 45
Appropriations Act, 11
assertiveness, 58
Austria, 39, 52, 60
authority, 5, 9, 14, 15, 22, 23, 28, 35, 36, 39, 42, 44, 45, 46, 56, 57
awareness, 15, 33, 48, 49, 58

B

background information, 19
Balkans, 3
barriers, viii, 2, 4, 13
Belgium, 8, 31, 39, 56, 58, 60
border control, 28
border security, 26
Bulgaria, 39, 60

C

CAP, 6, 29
censorship, 31
challenges, 3, 4, 42, 57
Chamber of Commerce, 14
China, 39, 55, 57
CIA, 54
Civic Democratic Party, 53
climate change, 4, 9
Cold War, 3, 10
communism, 52
Communist Party, 53
conflict, 4
congressional offices, 30
consent, 46, 47, 57, 60
Consolidated Appropriations Act, 11
constituents, 9, 29
Constitution, 60
control measures, 28
convergence, 14
cooperation, vii, 2, 3, 4, 6, 9, 12, 13, 14, 15, 19, 20, 21, 25, 28, 29, 32, 34, 36, 43, 45, 57, 59
coordination, 6, 9, 12, 17, 18, 22, 24, 29
corporate governance, 6
Council of Ministers, viii, 7, 9, 23, 41, 42, 44, 45, 46, 48, 55, 56, 57, 59, 60
Council of the European Union, viii, 7, 9, 41, 44
Cyprus, 39, 60
Czech Republic, 39, 53, 60

Index

D

decision-making process, 11, 39
delegates, 16, 17, 21, 25, 26, 27, 29, 30, 35
democracy, 3
Democratic Party, 53
Denmark, 39, 60
dialogues, 14, 59
direct investment, 3
draft, 23, 47, 55, 56

E

economic downturn, 3
economic integration, 13, 14, 15, 36
economic partnership, vii, viii, 1, 11, 41, 43
economic relations, 12, 14, 15
economics, 7, 51
election, 48, 49, 54, 58
embargo, 57
energy security, 4, 6, 54
environment, 7, 8, 45, 52, 53, 54
environmental degradation, 3
equality, 19, 51
Estonia, 39, 60
EU legislation, viii, 6, 7, 8, 9, 21, 23, 33, 41, 42, 45, 55, 56
Eurasia, 18
Europe, 3, 8, 9, 10, 12, 13, 16, 20, 33, 34, 35, 43, 50, 51, 52, 53, 58, 59, 60, 61
European Commission, viii, 7, 9, 20, 23, 24, 41, 44, 47, 48, 56, 57, 59
European integration, 3, 43, 52
European Union, iv, vii, viii, 1, 3, 4, 7, 9, 10, 11, 23, 32, 39, 41, 43, 44, 60
executive branch, 22
exporters, 6
exports, 3

F

Farm Bill, 6, 29
FDI, 3
financial, 3, 5, 6, 26, 31, 32, 34, 42, 44, 47, 49, 51, 54, 55, 57, 60
financial crisis, 51, 55
financial data, 5, 42, 57
financial markets, 3
financial stability, 26
Finland, 39, 60
food products, 4
food safety, 26
force, 4, 5, 7, 42, 43, 44, 46, 48, 60
foreign affairs, 55
foreign direct investment, 3
foreign policy, 4, 7, 10, 18, 21, 42, 44, 45, 54, 57
formal exchange between Congress, vii, 1
France, 8, 39, 52, 53, 56, 58, 60
funding, 46, 52
funds, 6, 14, 16, 22, 33

G

Germany, 8, 39, 49, 52, 53, 60
governments, 44, 45
Greece, 39, 60
gross domestic product (GDP), 3
guidance, 14, 28, 29

H

harmonization, 26, 58
homosexuality, 49
House of Representatives, vii, 1, 9, 19, 29
human right, 52, 54, 55, 57
Hungary, 39, 52, 60

I

immigration, 45
imports, 3
independent members, viii, 8, 41, 50, 52
India, 55
infrastructure, 46
institutions, 2, 5, 7, 10, 11, 20, 27, 33, 36, 39, 42, 43, 44, 54, 57

integration, 3, 13, 14, 15, 36, 43, 52
international parliament-to-parliament relations, viii, 8, 42
international trade, 13
Iran, 3, 4, 55
Iraq, 4
Ireland, 39, 53, 60
Israel, 55
Italy, 39, 52, 53, 60

J

jurisdiction, 18, 22, 28, 29, 35

K

Kosovo, 18

L

Latin America, 39
Latvia, 39, 60
law enforcement, 3
laws, viii, 24, 41, 43, 56
leadership, 10, 14, 23, 27, 32
legislation, viii, 5, 6, 7, 8, 9, 12, 15, 21, 22, 23, 24, 27, 31, 32, 33, 41, 42, 44, 45, 54, 55, 56, 60
legislative authority, 23
legislative proposals, 30, 31, 50, 55, 57
Lisbon Treaty, viii, 2, 4, 5, 7, 9, 14, 36, 39, 42, 43, 45, 46, 47, 48, 49, 56, 57, 58, 60
Lithuania, 39, 60

M

Maastricht Treaty, 45
market economics, 51
marketplace, 13, 14, 36
Middle East, 39

N

national income, 46, 60
national interests, 58
national parties, 52
nationality, viii, 8, 41, 50, 58
NATO, 16, 55
negotiation, 5, 14, 57
Netherlands, 39, 52, 60

O

Obama Administration, 4, 24
officials, vii, 1, 5, 6, 10, 13, 20, 36, 56
operating costs, 32
OSCE, 33
oversight, 7, 14, 19, 22, 35, 48, 57

P

peace, 3, 8, 43, 58
personal relations, 10, 17, 24
Poland, 39, 52, 53, 54, 60
policy, vii, viii, 1, 4, 6, 7, 9, 10, 12, 18, 21, 22, 23, 28, 36, 39, 41, 42, 43, 44, 45, 54, 57, 58
policymakers, 5, 10, 12, 20
political appointments, 57
political party, 50, 53, 60
politics, 51, 52
population, 8, 49, 60
Portugal, 39, 60
presidency, 13, 54
president, viii, 5, 8, 19, 20, 42, 44, 48, 54, 60
proliferation, 3
prosperity, 3, 43
public awareness, 48, 58
public interest, 42
public policy, 12

R

ratification, 39, 49
recession, 51
reform, vii, 1, 5, 6, 12, 39, 42, 43, 54
regulations, 6
regulatory agencies, 13
regulatory oversight, 35
regulatory reform, vii, 1
resolution, 12, 16, 20, 39, 59, 61
rights, 5, 49, 51, 52, 54, 55, 57
Romania, 39, 60
Russia, 18, 39, 55

S

safety, 18, 26, 29
Sarbanes-Oxley Act, 6
security, 3, 4, 6, 18, 21, 26, 29, 31, 39, 45, 54, 55
Senate, 2, 5, 12, 16, 19, 21, 22, 23, 25, 26, 28, 30, 32, 33, 34, 35, 37, 38, 49, 59, 60
Senate Foreign Relations Committee, 34, 35
Single European Act, 45
Slovakia, 39, 60
social policy, 7, 45
social security, 39, 45
Spain, 39, 52, 53, 60
stability, 3, 26
state, viii, 4, 7, 8, 9, 20, 33, 39, 41, 42, 43, 44, 45, 46, 48, 49, 50, 51, 54, 55, 57, 60
supply chain, 21
Sweden, 39, 60
symbolism, 58

T

tariff, viii, 2, 4, 13
taxation, 7, 44
technical support, 8, 56
terrorism, 3, 5, 42, 54, 57
terrorist attack, 3, 15, 57
trade, viii, 2, 3, 4, 5, 9, 13, 14, 42, 44, 46, 57
trade agreement, 9, 46
Transatlantic Economic Council (TEC), vii, 2, 4, 10
Transatlantic Legislators' Dialogue (TLD), vii, 1, 4, 11, 14, 19, 59
transparency, 18, 39, 43, 58
treaties, 23, 43, 44, 59
turnout, 42, 49, 58

U

United Kingdom (UK), 39, 52, 53, 60
United States (USA), 1, 3, 4, 5, 9, 10, 11, 12, 13, 16, 24, 26, 29, 33, 34, 39, 42, 55, 57, 59, 60

V

value added tax (VAT), 60
veto, 5, 56, 57
Vice President, 5
vote, 5, 8, 23, 24, 47, 48, 49, 50, 51, 52, 54, 55, 56, 57, 58
voting, 45, 51, 58, 60

W

Washington, 2, 19, 20, 27, 29, 32, 33, 36, 39, 60
weapons, 3
White House, 14
withdrawal, 53
workers, 3
working groups, 26
world trading system, 3